MW00651733

Who Is a Worthy Mother?

Who Is a Worthy Mother?

An Intimate History of Adoption

Rebecca Wellington

University of Oklahoma Press : Norman

This book is published with the generous assistance of Edith Kinney Gaylord.

Library of Congress Cataloging-in-Publication Data

Names: Wellington, Rebecca Christine, 1975– author.
Title: Who is a worthy mother? : an intimate history of adoption / Rebecca Wellington.
Description: Norman : University of Oklahoma Press, [2024] | Includes bibliographical references and index. | Summary: "While reckoning with the pain and unanswered questions of her own experience as an adoptee and mother, author Rebecca Wellington draws on historical research to explore broader issues surrounding adoption in the United States, including changing legal policies, sterilization and compulsory relinquishment programs, forced assimilation of babies of color and Indigenous babies adopted into white families, and other liabilities affecting women, mothers, and children"—Provided by publisher.
Identifiers: LCCN 2023034426 | ISBN 978-0-8061-9370-0 (hardcover)
Subjects: LCSH: Adoption—United States—History. | Motherhood—United States—History.
Classification: LCC HV875.55 .W467 2024 | DDC 362.7340973—dc23/eng/20231122
LC record available at https://lccn.loc.gov/2023034426

The paper in this book meets the guidelines for permanence and durability of the Committee on Production Guidelines for Book Longevity of the Council on Library Resources, Inc. ∞

Copyright © 2024 by the University of Oklahoma Press, Norman, Publishing Division of the University. Manufactured in the U.S.A.

All rights reserved. No part of this publication may be reproduced, stored in a retrieval system, or transmitted, in any form or by any means, electronic, mechanical, photocopying, recording, or otherwise—except as permitted under Section 107 or 108 of the United States Copyright Act—without the prior written permission of the University of Oklahoma Press. To request permission to reproduce selections from this book, write to Permissions, University of Oklahoma Press, 2800 Venture Drive, Norman OK 73069, or email rights.oupress@ou.edu.

1 2 3 4 5 6 7 8 9 10

Contents

I dedicate this book to my polestar, my sister, Rachel, and my fiercely courageous daughters, Maria and Victoria.

Acknowledgments

Writing is a solo journey, but all stories are inspired and informed by many people, relationships, and interactions that give the story shape and meaning. One of my professors used to say, "When we write we are standing on the shoulders of giants who have come before us." There are so many amazing giants I am grateful for who have provided their shoulders to stand on along the way. This journey began as a small wave that nudged me to step out into the water when Dawn Hardison-Stevens told me my grand-mothers had come to her at 4 A.M. to say they were looking for me. Because of Dawn's hope and encouragement, I began writing. The very first person to lay eyes on my early writings about adoption was Colby Lamson-Gordon. For years her story as a transnational, transracial adoptee informed my own understanding of the impact of adoption on identity. I am incredibly indebted to her for trusting me with her story and for listening to mine.

When Alessandra Jacobi-Tamulevich at the University of Oklahoma Press came to me with an interest in my story, I cast off lines and truly began this voyage. Since then, Alessandra has been a patient and solid voice of knowledge, helping to steer me through the many unknown waters of book publishing. Without her wisdom and incredible foresight, this book would not be possible.

Once I began to make way and head to open waters, Sarah Newcomb provided much-needed proofreading and line editing for early drafts. I am especially grateful for Sarah's willingness to share her own Indigenous wisdom on Native Alaskan perspectives on family and belonging. Her combined feedback on both editing and content in the early stages of this book helped set the heading for this journey. As the book voyage gathered way, I started plotting my course of merging adoption stories from the past into my own experiences as an adoptee and mother. I was immensely inspired by the women who have navigated expeditions of adoption storytelling before me. Susan Devan Harness, Sandy White Hawk, Nefertiti Austin, and Nicole Chung are gallant explorers in the genre of adoption and motherhood memoir writing, and I am so grateful for their generosity, grace, and kindness in sharing their experiences and providing feedback on my writing. Marisa Antonaya provided incredibly detailed and swift line editing and proofreading for the final drafts and helped make it possible for me to complete the full manuscript in preparation for peer review. I am also incredibly grateful for the impeccable work of the editors at University of Oklahoma Press who helped prepare the final version of this book.

I would have struggled mightily along this entire journey if it were not for my sisters- and mothers-in-spirit, who listened patiently to me, held my hand, and read drafts of my writing, even when the story was totally adrift. With them on board I knew I wasn't alone. There are so many to thank, but I must recognize Armene Boatright, Karen Balog, Coco Wellington, Vanessa Suresh, Amy Keljo, Mary Verbovski, Katja Koehnlein, and Lisa Reibe for their honest, diligent feedback and love.

All along this journey, as I steered through unknowns, as doubts and the persistent waves of fear doused my confidence, I held tight to my binnacle, my steadfast guides always leading me safely, my husband, Bill Wellington, and my daughters Maria and Victoria. Their unwavering love and unconditional trust in me have taught me to trust myself as I journey farther and farther out to sea. My love and gratitude for them is immeasurable. Lastly, but most importantly, the reason I wrote every single page of this book was for my sister, Rachel. She is my North Star, the reason I picked myself up after every setback and the first person I thank in my heart with every triumph. It is my greatest hope that through this book, women, mothers, and adoptees can find healing and peace and that Rachel's blazing spirit, wherever she may be, can know that she is the catalyst for great, beautiful change.

Abbreviations

AAIA	Association on American Indian Affairs
AFDC	Aid to Families with Dependent Children
ALMA	Adoptees' Liberty Movement Association
BIA	Bureau of Indian Affairs
CAS	Children's Aid Society
CC	Catholic Charities
CUB	Concerned United Birthparents
CWLA	Child Welfare League of America
FNRI	First Nations Repatriation Institute
HEW	Department of Health, Education, and Welfare
HHS	Department of Health and Human Services
IAP	Indian Adoption Project
ICE	Immigration and Customs Enforcement
ICWA	Indian Child Welfare Act
IHS	Indian Health Service
NABSW	National Association of Black Social Workers
NASW	National Association of Social Workers
TANF	Temporary Assistance for Needy Families

UNCRC   United Nations Convention on the Rights of the Child

UNICEF United Nations International Children's Emergency Fund's

USCB   United States Children's Bureau

Introduction

Ancestors

We acknowledge that everything that we know that feels like knowing is because someone who loved us taught it to us.

Linda Tuhiwai Smith, Eve Tuck,
and K. Wayne Yang

A sea anchor is a gigantic fabric balloon set from the bow of a boat in stormy seas. It is designed to stabilize the boat in massive waves that could otherwise rip the vessel apart and pull it under, never to be seen again. The sea anchor itself is a paradox. It is meant to decelerate and stabilize a vessel; but unlike a traditional anchor that drops to the sea floor and digs into solid earth, a sea anchor uses the wild, churning sea itself as a stabilizing force. And unlike a traditional anchor, made of heavy metal with sharp flukes that dig and pin themselves under rock and mud, the sea anchor is flimsy, malleable like a parachute. But when half submerged at the surface of a rough sea, this flimsy balloon becomes big as it fills with water and slows a struggling vessel, giving the crew time to breathe, gather forces, take in sail, and survive the duration of a storm.

I know what it is like to be at sea in a storm. After graduating college I joined as a trainee on a sailing ship bound for a two-year voyage around the world. I joined the ship's crew in the home port of Lunenburg, Nova Scotia, Canada, in early fall of 1997. For a month we painted, chipped rust, sewed sails, crossed yards, and prepped our ship—an otherworldly combination of a century-old, 170-foot clipper haul fitted with a newly built three-masted barque sailing rig. As fall progressed, temperatures dropped, prolonging our stay at the dock; stormy weather closed in; and multiple planned celebratory castoffs were canceled because of storm warnings. Our chances of a safe departure diminished. In late October, under pressure to get the voyage off the ground, the captain took a risky gamble and decided on a departure date. Despite our weeks of painting, scraping, and bonding in the local pub, we were an untested crew on an untested rig. And we were sailing out into a full-blown North Atlantic gale. Our first night at sea we steamed south down the North Atlantic in forty-mile-an-hour winds, taking towering seas over the stern quarter of the ship. Through the night the ship swung, dove, and climbed wildly, pitching and rolling twenty to thirty degrees minute to minute. Crossing the deck to stand watch or use the bathroom meant at times literally crawling on hands and knees, inching along, and holding tightly to anything solid a frozen, wet hand could grasp as hundreds of gallons of icy sea water surged across deck.

We had no lifelines rigged on deck. Over half the crew was violently seasick and hardly able to function. Those of us who could function to stand watch were paired up with a buddy, to keep an eye out for someone going overboard. I didn't eat the day of our departure because I was so full of excitement and nervousness for the start of this insane voyage. With the benefit of an empty stomach, I evaded sea sickness that first night out. As I climbed up to the quarterdeck to stand my first night watch, I felt like I was clambering over the scaffolding of a swinging construction crane, holding on for dear life in the middle of complete darkness, aware only of the wailing wind and stinging sea spray. When I made it up to the deck, crouched low, white knuckling the pin-rail as the ship bucked and swayed, I saw my watch crew and watch leader huddled behind the ship's stack house, a mediocre shelter from the howling wind. Our watch leader, the able-bodied seaman, or AB, was a young man who had clocked hundreds of hours at sea, was coast guard certified, and understood the magnitude of what we were experiencing. He screamed for me to move slowly, stay low, and hold on. Fifteen feet below, on the other side of the rail, was the black, roiling North Atlantic Ocean, rushing past the hull of the ship. The AB's face was white and drained, and as he looked at all of our naive faces staring at him from under the wide brims of our soaked and bent sou'westers, he yelled loud enough to be heard over the wind, telling us to quickly and deliberately drive our marlin spikes into our eye sockets if we went overboard. The ship wouldn't be able to get us, and it'd be a better death than slowly drowning.

Just hours after this gruesome warning to stay on board at all costs, a fellow sailor on the next watch lurched for the railing of the ship to vomit. At that exact moment the stern was kicked high by a massive wave, and she was sent flying into the air, fortunately landing inboard of the bulwark, just barely missing getting swept overboard. But as she landed on deck her foot crashed down on a huge metal bit next to the railing and broke violently in multiple places. The sailor, writhing in tremendous pain, was carried down belowdecks where the ship's doctor attempted to set and splint her foot, which was now not below her ankle but to the side of her leg. As the doctor worked to stabilize the sailor's foot, both she and the sailor were pinned down for stability by other crew members as the rocking haul threatened to slam them both against the sides of the sailor's bunk. Our ship turned north, altering course almost exactly 180 degrees, and headed toward Halifax, the closest port with a major medical facility. Halifax is forty miles up the coast *north* of Lunenburg. We were now going past our departure point, in the exact opposite direction of our plotted course and sailing deeper into the gale.

Through the rest of the night our ship clawed its way back north, sailing directly into oncoming weather, climbing and then diving into the relentless waves. In the morning light of the next day, we rounded into Halifax harbor to see an ambulance waiting for us on the dock, ready to transport our crewmate to the hospital. As I watched her being carried by stretcher into the ambulance, I knew two things about this voyage. One, the ship was our lifeline. Our lives depended on it, literally. We needed to stay onboard it and we needed it to stay afloat. Second, to keep our ship safe, upright, and moving forward, in order to make this journey happen, we all had to lean in and support one another as a crew, whether that meant deploying sea anchors to steady our ship or sailing directly into a storm to get an injured crewmate to safety. Nobody could do this alone. For the next two years, the ship became my home, and the crew became the family that would carry me safely through rough seas. In the morning light of that second day of our journey, at the dock in Halifax, I understood these two points clearly. But I did not yet know that this ship and its crew, like a sea anchor stabilizing me in a storm, would come to fill a void in my life, a void I wasn't fully aware existed.

I was adopted at birth through a closed, private adoption process that kept the transaction of my tiny baby body from one family to the next totally secret and sealed away. It is time to tell this story, not just mine but that of millions of American adoptees whose births and lives have been shrouded in secrecy and shame, leaving a toxic void in our nation's collective memory. The history and policies around adoption matter, even to those who aren't adopted. Nearly everyone in America is affected by adoption. Some experts estimate that six out of ten Americans have a direct, intimate connection to adoption. An estimated five million Americans alive in 2015 were adopted. From a macro view, adoption is the lens through which we can see in stark relief how our nation differentially values humans. The whole project of adoption is contingent on making value judgments about a pregnancy—about who is a worthy mother and who is a worthy baby. In legal arguments heard in the Supreme Court case of *Dobbs v. Jackson Women's Health Organization*, Justice Amy Coney Barrett suggested that adoption could render the issue of abortion irrelevant. Justice Samuel Alito echoed this same sentiment in his 2022 opinion overturning the 1973 *Roe v. Wade* decision, in which he justified abolishing abortion rights by arguing that "the domestic supply of infants relinquished at birth or within the first month of life and available to be adopted has become virtually nonexistent."[1] This strategy of using adoption as a cudgel against reproductive rights involves a dangerous and duplicitous logic. Instead of affirming parenting and motherhood, as Barrett claims it does, this logic affirms the shame of fertility by imposing the burden of forced pregnancy on women, thus stripping them of their autonomy regarding fertility. Most damaging, it upholds the assumption that it is a woman's destiny to produce children and raise them within the narrow confines of hegemonic motherhood.

Our nation has now entered a post-*Roe* world, the implications of which are staggering for all Americans. If we want to critically unpack motherhood and womanhood in America at this precarious turning point, we must include our complicated history of adoption. This book is a critical analysis of our nation's past and present relationship with adoption, fertility, and motherhood, framed through my personal narrative as an adoptee, a mother, and a historian. The sea and sailors' experiences at sea are metaphors that I draw on to define my journey through adoption and motherhood. The wild precariousness of sea voyaging is an especially prescient metaphor at this moment in American history, when women's value and identities are being thrashed in a political storm surrounding American identity itself.

I know nothing about my biological father; what I know about my biological mother is scattered and uncertain. This not-knowing was nearly debilitating for me. For years, to keep myself upright and to stabilize myself, and as a reprieve from the storm, I used my adopted family history—my parents, grandparents, and their ancestors' stories of immigration, survival, endurance, and relentless courage—to fill my sea anchor.

In high school, I started to learn about the Holocaust and World War II. The immediate role my adoptive parents' families played in this history mesmerized me. These were such profound stories of survival and courage, and I desperately needed them. I began to fill my sea anchor with my adoptive parents' ancestral stories, and I pulled myself close to them so they could fill me with meaning and purpose. These stories over the years have billowed out, filling a void in my past, and have steadied me in a churning sea of unknowns. As a young adult, I took these stories on as my own, anchoring myself to them to root my past and add meaning to why I'm here and what I'm supposed to do with this life I have. For a long time, this was how I attempted to fill my identity: with stories of people I've known and known of but to whom I'm actually not physically or biologically connected. The foundation of my connection to these people is the fast-moving, churning water. It is not solid, yet it is compelling and powerful. I hold the line of my sea anchor tight, but these ancestral stories are not mine and they no longer fill and stabilize the anchor I need in stormy seas.

For most of my life, I believed that my adoption was easy, insignificant, and unimpactful to my family and me. When I was a young child, I would daydream about my birth parents. I dreamed that they were royalty, that I was of royal blood, and that there was some beautiful, ornate castle I was meant to be living in. Deep in my heart, I knew this wasn't true. But not knowing was also a comfort in a weird, painful way. It allowed me the latitude to believe that I came from greatness. I could paint any picture I wanted of my ancestors and then live in that fantasy. It was great to have these fantasies, but there was always emptiness at the end. Even if my people were brilliant, gorgeous, intelligent, and noble, they weren't part of my life, and I wasn't part of theirs. They left me. In my childhood fantasies, I was always stuck wrestling with this dilemma. If they were so great, how could they leave me? Being adopted felt like wearing a shameful *A* emblazoned on my chest and heart, like the one Hester Prynne was forced to wear in *The Scarlet Letter.*

Although I grew up trying to convince myself that my adoption was insignificant, I also knew in my heart that being adopted was embarrassing and uncomfortable to talk about. My birth mother, the woman who grew me inside her belly for nearly ten months, didn't want me or couldn't keep me. My conception and life were an accident. That is a heavy cross to bear. I grew up believing that this also meant that my adoptive parents were committing a brave act of community service by bringing into their homes an unwanted baby, an unplanned life. But this all meant not having any real anchors in my life. I knew this immediately from my earliest memory, at the age of about four, when I saw the look on my teacher's face and my friend's parents' faces when they learned I was adopted. It was the look of pity. And inevitably, the words that followed this gut reaction of pity were words of admiration for my parents. And behind those words was the message of sacrifice. My adoptive parents had sacrificed their lives to help me out. This sequence of reactions and comments would play out again and again and again throughout my childhood— shock, pity, then admiration. I was a passive agent in all of it. I was the rejected baby bravely taken in by my adoptive parents, heroes who stepped in to clean up the shameful mess left by my irresponsible birth mother. My own actions weren't shameful, but my existence was.

And so I spent large parts of my early childhood carefully building fantasies of what my life would have been like if I hadn't been adopted. I took great artistic license in these fantasies. There were castles and ponies and gardens and silk gowns. But what there wasn't, ever, in these fantasies was shame. In these birth family fantasies, I was wanted, I was planned, I was meant to be part of the family. These people looked like me, and I looked like them. We had similar thoughts, and we liked similar things. Everything was meant to be. As I grew older, I could no longer trick myself with these fantasies. The castles and ponies became ridiculous in my mind. The fantasy lost its veneer because I became ever more aware with each year that passed that it was just that—a fantasy. By the time I was in middle school, I had begun looking around for other stories, real ancestral stories, to fill my sea anchor. Middle school was the time when kids were being asked to write reports, and family histories took center stage. I couldn't get away with writing pure fiction for my seventh-grade social studies teacher, claiming that Princess Diana of Wales was my real mom. I had to face reality. I began to assume my adoptive parents' ancestral stories of courage and survival, even though my connection to these family histories felt disingenuous, foreign, and not truly mine.

My adoptive father was born in Rutherford, New Jersey, in April 1942, four months after senior Nazi officials gathered at the Wannsee Conference in Berlin, Germany, to discuss the Final Solution, the Nazi plan of mass genocide of all Jewish people. My father's great-grandparents on both sides were Ashkenazi Jewish refugees from Kyiv, Ukraine, who escaped the oppressive pogroms in what was then part of the Russian Empire. Violent raids and massacres targeting Jewish businesses and homes became more and more common in Russia and Europe in the late 1800s and early 1900s, as anti-Semitism spread like wildfire and culminated in Adolf Hitler's Final Solution.

In the United States, my father's ancestors built successful businesses, creating with their own hands—first in their small, tenement home factories and later in thriving commercial buildings. They were innovators, builders, and creators, but most of all, they were survivors. They had fled a system that targeted them as inferior outsiders, burned their businesses, and ostracized their children. Their struggles and perseverance are the embodiment of the immigrant spirit. My father's great-grandparents on his mother's side emigrated to New Jersey in 1850. By the turn of the twentieth century, my grandmother's grandfather had built and owned a turn-of-the-century skyscraper in New Jersey. At this time, a fourteen-story building was considered a skyscraper and an architectural accomplishment. This familial history always astounded my grandmother—that her grandfather could excel so quickly as a new immigrant, barely able to speak English, and yet able to build skyscrapers in America. His wife would walk from apartment to apartment, collecting rent. One renter had a cigar factory in their tenement apartment. Through this regular exchange of rent collection, friendship and comradery developed, and later the two families would merge. The daughter of the land-lord and the son of the cigar makers would marry. These were my grandmother's parents.

My father's grandparents on his father's side immigrated from Kyiv in the late 1890s, several decades after my grandmother's ancestors. My grandfather was born in Manhattan in 1907, the first-generation child of Ashkenazi Jewish refugees, who, like my grandmother's family and so many other refugees, were deter-mined to forge a life and a world where their Jewish children could thrive. And thrive they did. My great-grandparents started a successful glove-making business, operated out of their tene-ment apartment in Manhattan. Their three children attended New York City public schools. Right out of high school, my grand-father went to New Jersey Law School, which would later become Rutgers Law School. His sister became a doctor, and his brother, like him, became an attorney.

Law school and then his work as an assistant prosecutor for Bergin County, New Jersey, brought my grandfather to my grand-mother's neighborhood. My grandparents met at Mountain Ridge

Country Club, a Jewish country club in South Orange, New Jersey. The club was one of several private golf clubs established around the United States in the early 1900s as a safe haven and community space for upper-middle-class Jewish families who had been blackballed by private clubs that excluded Jewish members. Like many second- and third-generation Jewish Americans, my grandparents wanted to assimilate into American culture. Their identity as Jews was central to their being. Yet, as Reformed Jews, they wanted to be both Jewish and American. Country clubs like Mountain Ridge offered a safe space for this hybrid identity. Here, members could live the American dream, play golf with friends on the weekends, gather for the weekly bridge game, and have elegant kosher meals in the dining room with friends and family. At clubs like Mountain Ridge, Jewish Americans could experience the American dream without being shunned, humiliated, and—worst of all—excluded.

When my father was five years old, his family left New Jersey, moving west to find cleaner air due to my grandmother's asthma diagnosis. Her doctor encouraged her to seek out healthier air quality in the American West, so my grandparents headed to Colorado. But what was intended to be a permanent move quickly ended after only six months. Upon their arrival in Colorado Springs, my grandparents sought membership at the local golf and country club, hoping to connect with a community similar to the one that had enriched their social and familial lives back in Rutherford. But in 1947, Colorado Springs did not have a golf club open to Jewish members. My grandparents were instantly turned away from all the local clubs. This time, before moving on, my grandparents did their research and learned that just a thousand miles farther west, in Los Angeles, was Hillcrest Country Club. Hillcrest was established in 1928, on 142 acres on the south side of Beverly Hills, as a Jewish-only club catering to Hollywood's Jewish leaders, innovators, and actors who were excluded from other society and industry establishments. By the 1940s, some of Hollywood's biggest stars, including George Burns, Jack Benny, Danny Kaye, and Al Jolson, could be found in the Hillcrest dining room smoking cigars and telling jokes. My grandparents packed up their recently unpacked boxes in Colorado Springs, got back in the car, and drove west to Los Angeles. Hillcrest was their beacon and would become their new home away from home.

As a child, I remember our Thanksgiving dinners being celebrated at the large round tables of the Hillcrest dining room, looking out the towering windows on the expansive golf course. Walking into the subdued club, I always felt intimidated by the space and the elegant, almost regal people who moved within it. During our Thanksgiving meals at the club, I would beg my sister, Rachel, or one of my cousins to go with me to the bathroom. I was certain that if I was caught in the gold-lit women's parlor room, with the soft pink marble floors and the thick white hand towels embroidered with the gold Hillcrest insignia, I would be identified as a nonmember, not classy enough, and kicked out the back door. My biggest fear was being identified as *not* Jewish. On the outside, I struggled to authentically fit in at Hillcrest because my mother was German Lutheran. That in itself presented a sizable barrier between me and authentic acceptance into the Hillcrest community. But beyond this was the fact that I wasn't even biologically related to my Jewish father. Ironically, what literally drove my grandparents across the American West to Hillcrest was the fact that there, in that immaculate, elegant space, they would *not* be kicked out. They would be welcomed, as Jewish Americans, with open arms. But I, their adopted granddaughter, with a German Lutheran mother, with no biological ties to my father and his brave Jewish ancestors who had fled the Kyiv ghettos a century earlier, didn't belong.

My adoptive mother was born in Göttingen, Germany, in 1944, eleven months before Adolf Hitler shot himself in the head as Soviet troops stood at the gates of the Reich Chancellery in

Berlin, and sixteen months before General Douglas MacArthur accepted Japan's formal surrender on the deck of the USS *Missouri* in Tokyo Bay. Her parents met while working together in the publishing house of Vandenhoeck & Ruprecht in Göttingen, a large university town in central Germany. My grandfather had been awarded a position in 1931, after working as an apprentice in Chemnitz and earning his journeyman's certificate from the chamber of commerce. He suffered from muscular dystrophy, a debilitating, cruel illness that started to afflict his body when he was a young man and just beginning his apprenticeship. My grandfather's dream was to become a publisher and bookseller, but his illness presented nearly unbearable obstacles.

By the time my grandfather earned a position at Vandenhoeck & Ruprecht, the Third Reich had begun infiltrating almost every facet of German life and society. Eugenics, the pseudoscience of improving the genetic quality of humans by weeding out people who were deemed racially and physically inferior and weak, was reaching its zenith in Europe and the United States. Eugenics not only would dictate American policies on intelligence testing and sterilization programs but also was quickly becoming one of Adolph Hitler's beloved doctrines and would become foundational to his Final Solution, the strategic mass genocide of Jewish people, orchestrated in the name of science and genetic cleansing. But Hitler's use of eugenics as a policy tool cut multiple ways, not just toward people considered racially inferior but also those considered behaviorally and physically inferior. My grandfather's muscular dystrophy would leave him weak and bedridden for weeks; it also left him at the mercy of Nazi doctors eager to please Hitler and prove that the sterilization and murder of those considered genetically weak were justified.

Multiple times, while my grandparents were a young couple working in publishing in Göttingen in the mid-1930s, my grandfather would be forced by the German health department to leave work and submit to multiday medical examinations by Nazi doctors. Although he never fully disclosed to anyone what happened during these examination periods, my grandfather would arrive home from them completely exhausted and traumatized. Using the justification of eugenics science, Reich policy dictated that anyone with a hereditary weakness was prohibited from getting married and having children. This created immense heartbreak for my grandparents, who were deeply in love and wanted to start a family. The Reich was also implementing sterilization protocols in government-run hospitals, and my grandfather was afraid that he would be forced to be sterilized because of his muscular dystrophy.

But in January 1942, shocking news came to my grandparents: my grandfather had been cleared of his inferior status as a genetic carrier of muscular dystrophy. Without questioning how this serendipitous ruling came down, and despite the horrific testing my grandfather had endured at the hands of the Nazis, my grandparents immediately got married. Within a year, they were expecting their first child, my adoptive mother. When my mother was born, Germany was in the final throes of the war. The nation was collapsing as British, French, American, and Soviet troops clawed their way into the country, beating down a now-starving, battered German army. My grandparents rented the small top floor of a large home owned by a university professor and his family, who inhabited the rest of the house. My grandparents were incredibly poor, like most Germans at that point in the war. Food was scarce. Unrelenting bombings, fires, mass destruction, and killing had decimated farms and gutted trade and movement of goods across the country.

Fifty years later, on my grandmother's eightieth birthday, my grandmother would learn how my grandfather had been miraculously cleared of his inferior physical status and given permission to marry and have a family. Gunther Ruprecht, who ran the publishing house my grandparents worked for, where they met and fell in love, had a close friend who was an influential, high-ranking

Nazi doctor in the Reich. At the risk of his own life, Gunther advocated for my grandparents, convincing his Nazi friend to draft falsified papers on their behalf, thus allowing them to marry and start a family. At my grandmother's eightieth birthday party, Gunther himself, now nearly one hundred years old, came to the celebration explicitly to share this long-held secret with my grandmother, mother, and aunt. Finally, fifty years after the horrors of the reign of the Third Reich; after the unrelenting fear the Gestapo spread across German society; after Hitler shot himself in the head, the Western allies carved up Germany into four quadrants, and the Soviet Union built a wall around eastern Germany; finally, in his last years of life, Gunther Ruprecht felt safe enough to share this secret with the people he had risked his life to help.

My adoptive parents are the babies and grandbabies of these courageous people who fought against incredible odds to do more than just live and survive; they sought to thrive and make a better life for their children. The serendipitous, unconventional union of these two people—a grandson of Ashkenazi Jewish refugees and a German Lutheran immigrant, children of fighters and survivors—opened a remarkable door for me. These were the people who took me in as a newborn. And these are the people whose stories filled my sea anchor. But as much as I grasped at the anchor line, my grip was weak, and the sea anchor, once full of other people's stories, began emptying into the wild sea. For most of my adult life, I've tried to connect to these histories, but I am neither German nor Jewish. And the paradox of these two cultural identities, the German Lutheran and the Jewish American, made it even harder to find footing. I learned German and studied in Germany while in college. I attended temple when I visited my Jewish grandmother and joined the Jewish student group in high school. But in all these spaces, I was a perpetual outsider, looking in through a glass wall I could not penetrate. I spent my childhood excessively jealous of my German and Jewish American cousins. They appeared to walk through familial life with incredible ease, their identities and place in the family culture unquestioned. I existed in this liminal space of being part of the family but not naturally fitting in.

The birth of my own daughters, followed in fairly quick succession by the death of my sister, fundamentally altered my understanding of adoption and burst the bubble of the two fantasies that I had tethered myself to throughout my life: first, that my adoption didn't matter; and second, that my adoptive parents' ancestral stories of courage and survival could fill the void of my unknown ancestral past, that these stories could give me meaning and purpose in life. I grew tired of relentlessly trying to convince myself of these things. These stories no longer held meaning. My grasp on the weathered line of the sea anchor was giving way.

Birth and death are the most consequential events in human experience. As they happen around us, to people we know and love, our worlds fundamentally change. The births of my two daughters seismically altered how I saw myself as an adopted person and now as a mother. I didn't want the fantasy anymore. I wanted the truth. Five years after my second daughter was born, my sister died. Her death shook me again, but on a different level: it threw into question all the assumptions and beliefs I had about my family at that point. The death of my older sister, Rachel, capsized the metaphorical boat that was my adoptive childhood family. Throughout my childhood, my sister was the one person who knew this secret: that being adopted was actually shameful. We never talked directly about it, but we talked and joked indirectly about it all the time. We had an unspoken code: we understood each other and had each other's back. I held on so tightly to my sister when we were young because she too knew the humiliation and subtle, persistent ache that came with being adopted. We would make endless jokes about our birth mothers and what it would be like if they had kept us.

Rachel's birth mother was fourteen years old when my sister was born. Rachel would tell elaborate stories about living in a trailer, being surrounded by cows, and having eighteen younger brothers and sisters at her ankles. My birth mother was in her early twenties and in law school when I was born. Rachel would joke that she was probably a famous politician who would ship me off to some boarding school in Switzerland and would be too busy to give me the time of day. Rachel and I thought these stories were hilarious. Telling them was like cutting into a semi-healed wound. It hurt, but there was some sick satisfaction in telling them. This was our way of getting back at our birth mothers. We ridiculed them. We insulted them. We wanted to tell them we were better off without them, that our adoption was the best thing that had ever happened to us. But we both knew that behind all that cruel hilarity, we were so hurt, so mad that they had left us. Rachel and I were partnered as rejects.

When Rachel died at forty-two, I felt more alone than I had in my entire life. A giant rift had grown between us in the years before her death, and we were not even on speaking terms in the months leading up to her death. But I knew she was out there, even though she was so far away. Years after our childhood, I still knew that my sister understood me and got me on a level that no one else did. She knew what it was like to carry around the shame of adoption and elaborate stories we would tell ourselves and others to cover up that shame. We had both spent our lives finding different ways to cover over and disguise the scarlet *A* of adoption that we carried on our chests. I spent my energy building a life in a fashion that I secretly thought my birth mother would be proud of and would approve of. My goal was to make her regret giving me away. My sister's strategy was just to burn everything to the ground so there was nothing left to be ashamed of. I dealt with my pain by working harder. Rachel dealt with hers by drinking harder, taking more pills, and dulling the pain while it ate her alive. When the pain and shame did catch up to Rachel, culminating in her death from a drug overdose, it felt to me as if all the decorations and distractions I had carefully spent years laying on top of my scarlet *A* to hide it from view were immediately ripped off. I was left standing naked, unmasked, and totally alone.

I could say that I was adopted because I was the result of an unplanned pregnancy and my birth mother felt she could not raise me. That is a simple explanation that I have given many times, including to my own children, when they ask why I was adopted and why I didn't grow in their grandma's belly. But it isn't that simple. There were so many forces, large and small, many of which I will never know, that contributed to the circumstances of my adoption.

Adoption practices are woven into the fabric of American society and are a direct reflection of how our nation differentially values humans, particularly mothers. As renowned adoption scholar E. Wayne Carp writes, "Adoption is a ubiquitous social institution in American society, creating invisible relationships with biological and adoptive kin that touch far more people than we imagine. Any social organization that touches so many lives in such a profound way is bound to be complicated."[2] Carp makes this claim about the significance of adoption in American culture, but he misses a fundamental point that determines normative assumptions about adoption—the ways we value mothers and women differ at various intersections of identity, including race and class.

Adoption has also operated for years as an anecdote for fixing broken families. Babies born to mothers who could not create— or were told they should not create—a solid family for a child to grow up in are adopted out. And partners who want children seek babies to adopt to make their families complete. But behind all of this are normative assumptions about what a solid and complete family is. Our national politics, economics, and social policies are based on an intransigent image of this family. This nuclear family requires a mother, a father, two or more children, stable housing, a nice front yard, and home-cooked meals. This image is still largely tethered to the Cleavers in the hugely influential 1950s TV show *Leave It to Beaver*. But the reality, on the ground and in real time, doesn't look much like the Cleavers at all.

The dominant, valued image of the American family, the *Leave It to Beaver* picture, is not only an outlier to what real American families look like. It is also heavily problematic and even toxic in how it runs contrary to reality. And adoption practices operate like a microscope, exposing the duplicity and toxicity of this normative American family narrative. Over the past sixty years, there has been a steady decline in the percentage of children raised by two parents. Today, nearly four in ten births are to single mothers or mothers living with a nonmarital partner. At the same time, household family structures are transforming to include multiple generations living together and children living in blended families, with stepparents and other guardians who are not biological parents. Marriage rates are the lowest they have been in the past sixty years, and divorce rates are at an all-time high.

People make families. Birth is an essential part of the creation of families. And birth rates are also dramatically shifting. In 1976, 40 percent of women ages forty to forty-four had four or more children. By 2014, that number had dropped to 14 percent. Birth rates in the United States are dropping dramatically. Family size is shrinking and changing. Yet there is one demographic in which we currently see a rise in birth rates. In 1960, only 5 percent of all births occurred outside of marriage, whereas by 2000, that number had climbed to nearly 25 percent. Within this group of babies being born outside marriage, virtually all the growth has been driven by increases in births by cohabiting women.[3]

As these family trends are dramatically shifting, so are adoption rates. At their absolute peak in 1970, 175,000 babies and children were adopted in the United States. By 2012, that number had dropped to 125,000. As the number of babies and children being adopted is decreasing, a larger percentage of those being adopted are being adopted by extended family members, many of whom are biologically related to the child.[4] The picture of the American family is changing. Yet normative assumptions about the American family and who has access to that narrative have failed to change.

My adoption story fits congruently with the data. I was born and adopted in 1975, when adoptions, especially adoptions into nonfamilial homes, were at their pinnacle. None of the members of my immediate family are biologically related to me. I have lived my life in a family pulled together by loose threads of legal connection, held together by contracts of adoption and marriage, not blood. Sometimes people choose to adopt children to fill a void in their lives and to fulfill the image of them as parents that society expects. In these circumstances, the adoption is about the parents, not the children. The child's job is to provide this image for the parents, to play a role so that parents can feel validated in their creation of the nuclear family that society has for decades reinforced as the backbone of success. This image—and the accompanying necessity of children to justify one's value and worth—is especially true for women.

To a certain degree, I believe this is the context in which I was adopted. My sister and I spent our childhood trying desperately to play the role of appeasing and pleasing children so that the family image was gratifying to my parents. Conversely, we also, at times, worked diligently and ruefully to defy this role, disrupting this normative image of family. This disrupting role was almost entirely the part my sister took on. She defied her role at every turn, and my parents, to a large degree, were ill-equipped to respond to her defiance. I now understand that all of us failed to see how my sister's actions stemmed from her suffering, shame, and pain. Most of my childhood was spent in a confusing paradox: a wholesome, united, and privileged family unit versus what I saw and felt on the ground on a daily basis—chaos, pain, and unending battles between separate and unconnected people. I spent much of my life pretending that we were an ideal of what a family should and could be through the power of adoption. This pretending and the consequential silencing of the truth destroyed my sister. Only in her death was she able to speak her truth to power.

Several years ago, while teaching at the University of Washington, I had a run-in that set me on the path of writing this book. I was rushing through the hall of the College of Education, preparing for my class, when my friend and colleague Dawn Hardison-Stevens came up to me and said something I will never forget. Her ancestors are Swampee Cree, Cowlitz, and Steilacoom. At the time of this encounter, my colleague was the program coordinator for the Native Education Program at the UW College of Education. Dawn had taught courses on Native history and Native knowledge in the College of Education and in the American Indian Studies Department. She was an active and passionate Indigenous activist for Pacific Northwest Indigenous rights and cultural heritage. Every quarter she would come and speak to my History of Education students about Native knowledge and how Native scholars and teachers were bringing Native knowledge and history into public schools in the Pacific Northwest region. Dawn would always start these talks by asking my students to think about their ancestors and where their people came from. She would ask, "Have you ever felt pulled to those places where your ancestors came from? Have you been to those places? Did they feel familiar, comfortable, like home?" As students shared their experiences, I would sit listening, feeling equally inspired, despondent, and isolated. I had nothing to share.

On that fateful day, Dawn stopped me, pulled me aside in the hall, and said, "Your grandmothers—your blood grandmothers, your people—came to me at 4 A.M. this morning. That is when the ancient spirits come to talk, at 4 A.M. They told me they are watching out for you. They are looking to connect with you." She then exhaled deeply, stared me in the eye, pulled up the sleeve of her shirt, and said, "Look! I have goosebumps! My hair on my arm is still standing up. Becca, they came and talked to me. They want to know you!" I stood stock-still, feeling waves of panic, hope, and nausea wash over me. I wanted to sit down and cry, right there in the middle of the cold, hard linoleum floor of Miller Hall, but I had to stand in front of sixty students in a lecture hall and teach a class in thirty minutes. I couldn't move, and I felt as though I was going to vomit. What was I supposed to do?

I don't know my people; most significantly, I cannot find them because of sealed adoption records. In the paradigm of many Indigenous peoples, that is problematic because that bloodline, that connection to the ancestors, is so significant to one's identity and life journey.

I am not Indigenous. I know that my biological ancestors came from Europe. But as I struggle to make sense of who I am with these minimal shards of information, I have come to find meaning and relief in Indigenous understandings of identity and ancestral connection. Through my academic research and writing about Indigenous student resistance to colonizing education in the Progressive Era, I have had the privilege of working with and learning from a number of influential Indigenous scholars. Their historical research, their personal stories, and their contemporary work of bringing Indigenous knowledge and ways of knowing into classrooms has deeply impacted my understanding of identity. It is because of people such as my friend and colleague Dawn Hardison-Stevens that I lean into these powerful Indigenous perspectives in order to make sense of my own journey as an adoptee.

So, what do you do when you don't know where you came from and who your people are? How do you mold meaning out of life when you are missing that ancestral connection? From an Indigenous perspective, land is central to identity. One's connection to a homeland roots one to one's people and past. This is why when many Indigenous scholars, elders, and leaders speak, they begin by calling honor to their homeland and their ancestors, recognizing the tribal affiliations of their ancestors. In many cases, this opening statement of positionality is first spoken in their Indigenous language and then translated into English. This reaching back to the past with honor and respect, and doing so in one's ancestral native language, is also an effort to keep Indigenous languages alive and sustainable. This intentional process of positioning oneself in relation to Native spaces and one's own ancestors is noteworthy and antithetical to the way most non-Native Americans introduce themselves. Most people introduce themselves by talking about what they are doing and what they are going to do, focusing on the future rather than the past.

Derek Taira, a historian at the University of Hawai'i–Mānoa, always begins his classes by positioning his family identity, naming his ancestors and their native lands. He then draws a right-side-up and an upside-down triangle on the board. The right-side-up triangle symbolizes a white, Western perspective on identity in which the individual, the top point of the triangle, is the defining point of identity. What the individual makes and connects to, moving through life, is symbolized by the widening bottom of the triangle, that which defines that person. In contrast, the upside-down triangle symbolizes an Indigenous perspective on identity. The top, wide part of the triangle symbolizes ancestral community, family, and land. This past leads down the triangle to the bottom point, which symbolizes the individual. Thus, from this Indigenous perspective, individuals are defined by their past. It is their ancestors who define them in this present moment. The presentation of this upside-down identity triangle was stunning to me because, for me, that top part of my upside-down triangle, which leads down to me, is completely empty. How do I shape my identity with an empty triangle?

As my friend shared, my grandmothers are watching me, looking for a way to reach out to me, to throw their sea anchors into my hands. They came at 4 A.M. to tell her this. But there is a wall between us, between my blood ancestors and me. My adoption was silenced. It was done in secret, at a time when it was normal practice to rewrite an adopted baby's birth certificate so that the birth itself could "pass" as if the adoption had never happened, to make it look like that baby was born to their adoptive parents. The past was literally rewritten so that when I was taken, at birth, from my birth mother and then handed, two days later, to my adoptive parents, the realities of my conception and birth had been erased. There is no trail of evidence.

In the following chapters, I investigate adoption policy and practices in America through the twentieth century, concluding with twenty-first-century debates around women's reproductive rights. The story is a critical, historical analysis of adoption in America, including changing adoption policies, sterilization and compulsory relinquishment programs, forced assimilation of babies of color and Indigenous babies adopted out into white families, and other forces that have impacted women, mothers, and babies. Each chapter is bookended with my personal and familial experiences. I use the chronology of my life journey—of being adopted, growing up in a family in which I was biologically related to no one, having my own biological children, and then enduring the death of my sister—as a frame for engaging in a critical analysis of how our nation has responded to, governed, monetized, and used adoption as a tool for regulating women's fertility.

Adoption can operate with integrity and in the best interest of all members of the adopting triad, including the birth family, the child, and the adopting family. I do not claim that biological bonds between family members always determine the health and sustainability of a family. Nature doesn't always trump nurture when it comes to the health and development of children and families. We are all influenced by both to varying degrees. Children and adoptive family members can develop bonds that, in some cases, are more impactful, sustainable, and healthy than biological bonds. Adoptions can save lives. But this necessitates adoption being done with full transparency and through choice, support, and free will on the parts of both the relinquishing mother and the adoptive family. And this is not the pattern of adoptions historically in the United States.

In chapter 1, I open with the circumstances surrounding my adoption, exploring the depth of secrecy and shame that shrouded this event. I have been told fragments of details that I think are true about my biological parents, but they have only led to dead ends. I do not have access to my original birth certificate, only a falsified one that has my birth mother's name redacted and my adopted mother and father listed. In this chapter, I also explore the early-twentieth-century adoption history that established a system of erasing and hiding original records to present a revisionist history of a child and a family. I trace the evolution of closed adoption policies across the United States that fed a larger national narrative around the shame and stigma of adoption and fertility.

In chapter 2, I begin with the stories of resistance and assimilation that my sister and I had to navigate within our family growing up as adopted children. Tattooing became a method of both resisting familial assimilation and asserting our own individual identities. In this chapter, I connect my personal experiences with familial conformity to the ways adoption has operated nationally as a vehicle of cultural assimilation. This chapter focuses on the US government's shifting Indian policy in the mid-1900s, which moved from assimilation through education toward assimilation through adoption with the Indian Adoption Project. This government project coincided with the forced relinquishing of Indigenous babies from biological families and the involuntary sterilization of Indigenous women. Assimilation through adoption as a less formal policy was also reflected in the late twentieth century during the exploding growth of international adoptions into the United States. As more and more white families were raising children who looked, in many cases, distinctly different from them, practices of acculturating to adopted children's native cultures worked paradoxically to reinforce normative assumptions about the ideal white American family.

Chapters 3 and 4 open with my personal experiences of becoming a mother, including the birth of my first daughter and the challenges I faced in motherhood. I connect my birth experience to the larger changes in adoption policy and trends emerging in the same decade I was born and the growth of transnational adoption through the Korean War and Operation Babylift at the end of the Vietnam War. Chapter 4 centers on a critical analysis of early-twentieth-century sterilization policies that targeted women, particularly Black and Brown women. Nationwide sterilization programs, which in some states existed as social welfare policy into the 1980s, impacted how young women could or could not mother, who was allowed to mother, and who was valued as a mother. These policies would deeply shape the American psyche, codify the idealized nuclear family suburban dream, and, conversely, shame and stigmatize unplanned pregnancy.

In chapters 5 and 6, I share my experience of losing my older sister to a drug overdose while I still had young children, and the healing journey her death set me on. My sister's experience of being adopted and then giving a child up for adoption becomes a launchpad for me to explore the role social welfare and especially social workers have played in facilitating and perpetuating abusive practices in adoption and family separation. I connect my personal experience with making meaning of my sister's death and my need to tell her story to broader national movements that blow open the truth behind adoption experiences and the courageous efforts various people and initiatives have created to reconnect adopted peoples and their families of origin and bring humanity to adoption practices.

In chapter 7, I pull my historical narrative on adoption and fertility into the present day, connecting it to the impact of the 2022 Supreme Court decision in *Dobbs v. Jackson Women's Health Organization*. I argue that the philosophy that has permeated adoption policy over the past hundred years, which emphasizes the needs and rights of adopting families over the needs and rights of birth mothers and their communities, is being reignited in this post-*Roe* era. The focus is on the fetus—at the expense of the birth mother, her community, and even the life of that child *after* it is born. According to the majority opinion in the *Dobbs* ruling, forcing women to carry babies to term and then give them up for adoption is not a problem. In fact, for both Barrett and Alito, it is a viable solution to the demands of the adoption market. Moving forward in the post-*Roe* era means fighting for reproductive rights, transforming our perceptions of motherhood, and blowing apart this binary of the good and bad mother. When we expand our perspective of who can mother, we step out of the destructive good-bad mother binary that has perpetuated abusive adoption practices for decades.

The historical foundation of adoption in the United States is defined by abusive practices that expose our culture's continuing deep distrust of women, particularly poor women and women of color, and the paradoxical threat and power women's fertility pose to hegemonic societal norms. Millions of women in this country have been told that they may not keep their babies, or have been forcibly sterilized so that they do not have more children. They have been resoundingly told they are unworthy of being mothers. At the same time, women repeatedly hear the message that they are unworthy if they choose not to mother or cannot have babies. American women live within the tension of this paradox, which allows only a small window of acceptable motherhood, acceptable womanhood. When adoption is used as a tool by which to legitimize some women as mothers and delegitimize others, it becomes profoundly traumatizing.

My journey, looking back at the deep roots and threads that have bound and shaped my adoption and motherhood experience in America, is my attempt to find answers and meaning as I toss and turn in a sea of unknowns. The histories and voices of thousands of women and children over the past hundred years provide context and meaning for why my adoption is shrouded in secrecy, why motherhood has been so challenging, and why my sister struggled mightily in her life, resisting the expectations of both womanhood and motherhood. Women have existed and do exist in this impossible paradox of societal shame surrounding both fertility and infertility, and adoption sits at the crossroads. This history has become my new sea anchor. It holds me upright and steady in a churning sea.

1

Adoption

Families are where we live our economic and social
relations, and in families formed by law the fiction
that families are "private," constituted in opposition
to "public," is laid bare as the fairy tale that it is.

Laura Briggs

I was born on June 29, 1975, in Northridge Hospital in Northridge, California. At that time, California state law mandated a
forty-eight-hour waiting period between a birth and the time adoptive parents could retrieve the newborn. For my first two days of
life, I had no name, no family. My adoptive parents told me years
later that when they came to pick me up on July 1, nurses recounted
how I had been left alone in a hospital bassinet in the nursery,
screaming for hours, virtually untouched except for diaper changes
and bottle feedings. I would spend a significant part of my infancy
screaming bloody murder. My gestation and birth were silenced. I
believe that infant me screamed so much because I was mad about
the circumstances of my birth. After being silenced and hidden, I
was now making sure that I was heard and seen. I wanted to be
known. I wanted to be heard! What little I do know about my birth
and adoption is all shrouded in this veil of secrecy that originated
in shame—a shame targeting my birth mother for making a

mistake, getting pregnant at a time in her life when she wasn't able or ready to be a parent. And a shame targeting her family for actions and outcomes they could not control, but feared their neighbors, friends, and community would judge them for.

My birth parents are nearly a blank slate to me. But there are a few things I do know. My birth mother was in law school when she became pregnant with me. It is remarkable that in 1975 she was pursuing law with the goal of entering politics because both these professions operate so visibly in the public sphere. Yet the shame of her unplanned and out-of-wedlock pregnancy shifted her into a space of silence and hiding. I have learned through degrees of separation—from my parents, who heard it from the lawyer who mediated the adoption, who heard it from my birth mother and her family—that my birth mother was encouraged to hide the pregnancy and give me up for adoption so that she could pursue her career. She had to endure secrecy and hiding to be allowed access to public visibility. One reality was hidden in order to live another.

This paradox was especially true in 1975, when women were, for the first time in our nation, enrolling in large numbers in law schools. This was also a tipping point for women in politics. In the Eighty-Seventh US Congress, 1961–1963, twenty women held seats—3.7 percent of the body. This was the largest percentage women had ever taken up in Congress and double what their representation had been just ten years earlier. In 1963, Justice Lorna Lockwood became the first woman elected to the Arizona Supreme Court and the first woman in the United States to serve as chief justice of a state supreme court. In 1965, Patsy Takemoto Mink became the first woman of color and the first woman of Asian-Pacific Islander descent in the House of Representatives. In 1968, Shirley Chisholm became the first Black woman to serve in Congress. In 1972, Chisholm would run for president in the Democratic primaries, the first woman—and woman of color— to do so in US history. In 1973, Yvonne Brathwaite Burke became the first woman to give birth while serving in Congress. And in 1974, Elaine Noble became the first openly gay candidate elected to the state legislature, serving in the Massachusetts House of Representatives for two terms, starting in January 1975—just five months before I was born.[1]

I was born in an era of many firsts for women. Still, the expectations and narrow lanes of acceptability must have been nearly crushing for these trailblazing women as they challenged the nation to rethink what it meant to work in law and politics as women *and* mothers. And so my birth mother had to walk a very thin line through her pregnancy, navigating this liminal and contested space. Her response to this tension was to hide her pregnancy and my birth in order to live and operate in a public, professional sphere: not as a mother but as a woman. Sealed adoption policies of the 1970s allowed her to legally make our connection as mother and daughter nonexistent.

Pursuing birth documents that could lead to my birth mother's identity would require me to petition a judge to unseal adoption documents. And even under current legal parameters, these documents cannot be unsealed except under extreme circumstances involving matters of life and death. Today, only ten states in the country give adoptees unrestricted rights to their original, unaltered birth certificates.[2] California is not one of them. There is a historical evolution of adoption policy that culminated in the circumstances of my adoption and explains why I am left knowing virtually nothing about my birth or my birth family—this connection between birth child and birth family strategically severed—and why a pernicious silence and shame persist around adoption.

The saying that blood is thicker than water continues to shape and dominate the American psyche in deeply influential, if not subconscious, ways. The real picture of the American family, on the ground, is changing dramatically. Families are bound by complex threads of connection. The false assumption of what an ideal family should look like negates the experiences of children and guardians living outside a two-parent, heteronormative, biological ideal. There is a steady decrease in the number of two-parent families and a continual increase in the number of children raised by just one parent, a mother or father, or extended family, including grandparents.[3] Yet the normative expectations around who qualifies as an acceptable family are dominated by a genetically linked archetype, so much so that "non-genetic family forms tend to be rendered abnormal, pathogenic and unworkable."[4]

Extensive research on infertile adoptive mothers in the 1980s revealed the particularly pernicious assumptions rooted in expectations around fertility and parenthood that continue to impact the experiences of adopted children and families. The outcomes of this research show various interwoven societal assumptions. One, biological ties are important for bonding and love; thus, adoptive families are considered second best. Two, because of their unknown past, adopted children are viewed as second-rate. And three, because they are not biologically related to their children, adoptive parents are not considered real parents.[5] I have felt these assumptions through unintentional microaggressions my entire life. I vividly remember playing with my daughter and her friend several years ago when my daughter made an aside comment about me being adopted. My daughter's friend, who was only seven years old at the time, stopped dead in her tracks, looked up at me, and said, "You are adopted and you tell people?! Why don't you keep that a secret?" She said this to me so honestly, innocently, and with sincere pity. Already at the age of seven, she fully understood the shame and stigma society had placed on adoption. And with her own sweet gesture, she wanted to protect me from that shame.

This pathologizing and stigmatization of adoption is so insidious that it has even impacted research. Over the past half century, most social scientific adoption studies have focused generally on the negative attributes of adoptees and adoptive families. Most of these studies have been conducted to determine factors that cause mental health problems in adopted children.[6] This focus on the pathology of adoption has become a self-fulfilling prophecy, perpetuating the stigmatization of adoption into the twenty-first century. In her 2000 article "Adoption, Family Ideology, and Social Stigma," Katarina Wegar takes this conclusion a step further, writing, "The failure to recognize adoption as a stigmatized social institution might explain why post-adoption services in general, and services that would help adoptive families to deal with issues surrounding stigmatization in particular, are not a standard part of the adoption process."[7] In the field of historical research, renowned adoption historian Wayne Carp echoes this same sentiment:

> In light of the richness of the topic, it is surprising that there have been no comprehensive histories of adoption in the United States and that scholars generally have neglected the topic. This lacuna results in part from the fact that the primary sources necessary for writing such a history—adoption case records—have been sealed by tradition and state law. For professional historians, this had been an almost insurmountable barrier: no sources, no history.[8]

Stigmatizing, shaming, and silencing adoption is the water we swim in. It is as much a part of American culture as apple pie.

The story of adoption in America, much of which, as Carp explains, has been deliberately silenced, is long and complicated. Untangling the complex threads and knots of this story reveals that it is precisely these restrictive assumptions about family and acceptable identity that have cloaked the narrative in shame. This is the start of my journey to look back through time and understand these threads of silence and shame that collectively fabricated my experience as an adoptee in America.

Adoption practices in America during the late 1800s and early 1900s were unregulated, and both the relinquishing and acquiring of babies and young children were chaotic, diverse, and, in many cases, horrific. Babies and children who were informally adopted out during this period fell into one of three categories: foundlings (abandoned infants), orphans, and illegitimate children born to unmarried parents. One common denominator among all these children was poverty. In fact, over half of the "orphans" placed in orphanages and other infant asylums were only half-orphans, meaning they had one living parent who simply could not afford to care for them. The second common denominator was that these children were white. Early private and state-funded orphanages and asylums refused to accept babies of color.[9] Out of necessity, Black, Brown, and Indigenous communities—largely defined by institutional racism and cultural tradition—had intricate networks of care for babies and young children who could not be raised by immediate parents. Extended families, tribes, and church communities operated as safety services, nurturing and raising young children of color within a wide net of community-based care.[10]

The last common denominator in these early adoption systems was that the villain in all these circumstances was the impoverished birth mother. She failed in her poverty, she failed in her pregnancy, and she failed in her childrearing. Destitute birth mothers were pigeonholed in an impossible paradox in which they were damned for getting pregnant at a time when birth control and reproductive health care were not safe or readily accessible, damned for giving birth, and also damned for relinquishing their babies. So vilified was the act of giving up a baby while poor that some social workers referred to the adopting out of babies by poor single mothers as "abortion after birth."[11]

Early locally run childcare institutions, such as the Washington City Orphan Asylum in Washington, DC, and the New York Children's Aid Society, facilitated taking children away from poor mothers instead of providing services to support families struggling in poverty. Mothers frequently came to these aid organizations seeking temporary childcare, citing as concerns "Salary too small to keep and care for them properly" and "I have no one to care of children while I am working."[12] In a phenomenal twist of irony, many of these women worked as domestic servants and wet nurses for wealthy women yet could not earn enough money to keep and care for their own children. These traumatizing acts of relinquishing their own babies and young children were almost always meant as a temporary reprieve while these mothers desperately sought options for more income. But these unregulated institutions frequently took it upon themselves to "save" these young children, particularly Catholic children of Irish and Italian immigrant mothers, by permanently farming them out to Anglo-Protestant middle-class families.

The New York Children's Aid Society ran one of the most efficacious and appalling operations of child separation in the late 1800s and into the 1920s, by transporting poor immigrant children via cattle cars out of urban slums and into farming communities in Pennsylvania, Ohio, and points farther west. Started by Yale Divinity School graduate Rev. Charles Loring Brace in 1853, the Children's Aid Society (CAS) aimed to rescue "poor and homeless children from New York City's crowded, dirty streets and to place them out west in good Christian families where they would be cared for, educated, and employed."[13]

The CAS sought out children deemed "unwanted" through asylums and prisons. Some were brought to the CAS by desperate, impoverished families who were told that their children would be able to return home once their families could financially provide for them. In one documented case, when a father returned for his daughter after temporarily placing her, he was told she had been "put out on a farm in Kansas." Again, many of these children were not given away permanently by choice. The CAS was even accused of stealing children from poor homes in the city when parents were out working. An estimated 47 percent of all children funneled through the CAS and sent off on orphan trains weren't even orphans; they were kids pilfered from poor, immigrant homes.[14] Even when representatives of the CAS and other childcare institutions claimed to have been given permission by parents to take children away, many of these verbal agreements were made in bad faith or without any semblance of understanding. Immigrant parents who spoke little or no English had no idea what was happening and never gave knowledgeable consent to having their children taken from them.

The orphan trains were not simply shipping unwanted or stolen immigrant children to loving homes on western farms so they could be cared for and nourished in healthy rural America. These children were being sent off to work as unpaid laborers. In this "placing out" system, children had to earn their keep in these farming homes by working in the fields and homes. Contracts between organizations like the CAS and families seeking children for work stipulated that children would work in exchange for food, shelter, and basic education. As the orphan trains traveled west, they would stop at rural churches along the way. The children were taken off the train and lined up on the platform to be bid on by local families. The children who were not selected were loaded back on the trains to travel to the next stop.[15] In a study of 827 indentured children in Wisconsin conducted between 1913 and 1917, only 36 percent of the children were eventually fully adopted by the families they worked for.[16] The younger the children, the more likely they would be fully accepted into the family as one of their own. So, although some children were eventually adopted out, the majority were simply sent to work temporarily as indentured laborers.

The system of placing out orphans mirrored the outing programs that ran in government-run off-reservation Indian boarding schools at this same time. In 1875, while an officer in the US Army, Lt. Richard Henry Pratt was tasked with overseeing the internment of incarcerated Indigenous men who had been captured by the US Army. Through these early experiences with educating, training, and assimilating Indigenous prisoners, Pratt became convinced that work, and work among white people, was essential to, as he famously wrote, "kill the Indian and save the man."[17] In the first year of the opening of Carlisle Indian Industrial School, the US government's first off-reservation Indian boarding school, Pratt initiated a system that would become an integral part of the school curriculum. In that opening summer of 1879, eighteen Indigenous children, all students at Carlisle, were distributed to the homes of white families on farms across Pennsylvania, tasked with working in the homes and laboring in the fields.

The educational project of placing Indigenous children in white homes and white-owned businesses to work predominantly menial labor jobs for minimal pay was called the "Outing Program." The intention, set by Pratt, was that Indigenous youth "mastered the English language, internalized the habits of industriousness, and generally speaking, acquired the everyday habits of civilized living."[18] Outing programs would become essential components of school programming at Carlisle and other off-reservation Indian boarding schools around the country, thus proliferating this Office of Indian Affairs policy that complete assimilation of Indigenous children necessitated an education deeply rooted in work, particularly work among white, Protestant families.

The placing-out program through the orphan trains operated in the same way. The primary intention was not to find loving homes for these immigrant orphans but to assimilate them into white American culture through labor. Reverend Brace was unapologetic in his approach to assimilating the "dirty, uncivilized" immigrant youth on the streets of New York. His goal was to transform these "little vagabonds and homeless creatures into decent, orderly, industrious children."[19]

The confluence of destitute poverty, lack of legal representation, and compounding bigotry against particularly Catholic immigrant families all facilitated a system that actively and effectively ripped families apart in an effort to fashion new and acceptable children and families. In the early 1900s, several decades into Reverend Brace's orphan train project, Catholic authorities and community leaders saw this targeted attempt to, in many cases, steal young children from immigrant Catholic families and ship them west to Protestant families as corrupt, immoral, and deeply damaging. And they began working with child welfare reformers to help end these unregulated abusive practices.

In 1912, the US Children's Bureau (USCB) was established by Congress. Nine years later, the Child Welfare League of America (CWLA) was founded. This set in motion a wave of increased government regulation of these chaotic and often abusive adoption practices. Emblematic of many Progressive Era policies and institutions, leaders in both the USCB and the CWLA leaned heavily on the belief that science, coupled with bureaucratic regulation, could save American children and the American family.

This new era of regulation also marked a transition in policy thinking that focused on keeping "natural" families together instead of breaking them apart. It suddenly became taboo to take children away from their biological parents. Constructing and regulating natural American families formed by blood as opposed to adoption became an American policy endeavor. And when biological families could not be formed, they would be constructed to look as "normal" as possible. The USCB's primary goal was to regulate how, when, and to whom babies and children were adopted. A paper published in 1920 by Catholic Home Bureau executive secretary Edmond Butler, in affiliation with the USCB, stated that "unless carried out in accordance with approved standards" of deliberate matching of a child to appropriate homes, unregulated adoption would add to the "thousands of human wrecks" also seeking charity and would be "responsible for destroying the future welfare of very many if not most of those intended to be helped."[20] The huge weight of responsibility for the American family and society in general lay at the feet of these new institutions. The era of orphan trains and pilfering children from asylums and poor immigrant homes was coming to an end, and a new era of strategically and scientifically constructing appropriate American families was beginning.

With this new emphasis on blood-related families, the adoptions that did take place were designed to make families look as natural, or biologically connected, as possible. For the first time, private, regulated adoption agencies were established, and many of them catered to wealthy elites who wanted to create families that could pass as natural. One of these private agencies was the Cradle, founded by Florence Walrath in 1923.

The wife of a wealthy, prominent Chicago attorney, Walrath devised the idea of making adoption into a lucrative industry when she strategically and successfully replaced a stillborn baby— born to her older sister—with a healthy foundling in 1914. She began receiving requests for babies from childless couples, and the idea for her private adoption agency was born. By 1930, the Cradle was so successful that it was known as the "supply station for Hollywood mother love," catering to A-list clients like George Burns, Bob Hope, Barbara Stanwyck, and Al Jolson, all of whom adopted babies through the Cradle.[21]

One of the keys to the Cradle's success was the meticulous matching of the baby to adoptive parents. Babies had to biologically match the race, religion, and even looks of the adopting parents. Jewish babies went to Jewish parents. Blue-eyed babies went to blue-eyed parents. This ensured that a family could pass through life as being natural, without the stigma of a public adoption. Children never had to question their membership in a family if there were no glaring physical traits that set them apart from the rest of the family. And adoptive parents could rest assured that children, or prying neighbors, would never ask about the real origins of the family.

Part of this new policy of regulated, private adoptions included developing strategic ways to keep the adoption transaction out of the public eye and shrouded in silence. Early-twentieth-century state laws, like Minnesota's 1917 Children's Code Act, weren't meant to prevent adoptees from seeing their birth records. Rather, their explicit goal was to keep the *public* from viewing the records. Because of the stigma of shame and scandal surrounding adoption and illegitimacy in the early twentieth century, lawmakers wanted to protect adoptive parents from potential blackmailers who might threaten to expose "unnatural" families and from public scrutiny and harassment.[22] During this time, the practice of sealing adoption documents was meant to shield both the child and adoptive parents from the shame and stigma of adoption. What is significant is that part of the impetus of these laws was a concern that adopting parents would be extorted for having an adopted child. This speaks to the enormity of the stigmatization around adoption: the paradoxical failure, as seen through the eyes of the nation, of an unplanned pregnancy on the part of the birth mother and the failure to form a biological family on the part of the adoptive parents. It was seen as a stain on all people involved and had to be concealed.

By 1930, a new initiative emerged at the behest of two Illinois state registrars, Sheldon L. Howard and Henry B. Hemenway. They encouraged states to issue new birth certificates for adopted babies. The idea behind this initiative was to essentially create a second, "official" birth certificate for a baby, one that did not have the classification of "illegitimate" on it. A second certificate would be created, naming the adopting parents as the birth parents. The original birth certificate, which named the birth mother and sometimes the birth father, if known, would be permanently sealed away, not just from the general public but also from the eyes of the adopting triad (the birth parents, baby, and adoptive parents). The impetus for this falsification of the official birth record was to wash away the sins of the child's birth, recasting the birth and creation of the adopting family as legitimate, acceptable, and natural. Howard and Hemenway characterized themselves as "missionaries, who should bring about the rectification of the existing evils" of children born out of wedlock and adopted out. They worried that the stigma and shame of adoption, if revealed openly on a birth certificate, would "permanently impair the otherwise peaceful mental conditions and happy lives" of both the adopted baby and the adopting parents. By 1948, nearly every state in the country had implemented Howard and Hemenway's initiative of sealed and altered birth records.[23]

A second reason state after state lined up to change their policies and embrace this sealed and altered records initiative was mistrust of the birth mother. The relationship between adoptive parents and birth mothers was suspect even with the earlier open and less regulated adoptions.[24] Falsified and incomplete records became standard in many states across the country, an attempt to create a barrier of secrecy and anonymity between adopting families and birth mothers. Alabama, for example, never fully sealed adoption records, but social workers would selectively withhold certain pieces of information about the baby in what they believed was the best interest of that child. In many cases, social workers deliberately did not tell adopting parents that a light-skinned baby's birth parents were Black or Native American. Thus, the stigma and shame of adoption were compounded for children and birth mothers of color.[25]

Policymakers and social workers were concerned that untrustworthy unwed birth mothers would try to insert themselves back into their children's lives and cause problems for the adoptive families. And as more states around the nation implemented secretive adoption policies in the post–World War II years, this policy of secrecy became more widespread and easier to enforce. By the mid-twentieth century, confidential adoption policies, or sealed adoptions, became standard. This also coincided with a massive national boom in adoptions. Private, confidential adoptions meant that birth mothers and adopting parents intentionally never met and were legally prohibited from having any contact.

Birth documents were altered to erase the existence of the birth mother.[26]

This was the policy under which I was adopted. The only birth certificate I have, the only official document recording my birth that I have access to, was created by a California state registrar four months after my birth. The only names listed on my birth certificate as my mother and father are those of my adoptive parents. There is no classification of "illegitimate." The altered document erases the existence of any other participants in my birth except for the attending physician. He and the now anonymous nurses who attended my birth are the only witnesses who could attest to the existence of another person present at the moment I came into the world—my birth mother. Legally, she no longer exists as a participant in my birth on the evening of June 29, 1975, at Northridge Hospital, in Northridge, California. My birth mother has been erased from my beginning.

Several key demographics within adoption transactions significantly changed in the 1940s and would mark a new era of adoption practices in the nation. First, most women giving babies up for adoption between 1948 and the 1970s were younger, with a median age of eighteen years, and were relinquishing their babies earlier, at four days rather than four years old, which was the median age in the early 1900s. Also, for the first time, the vast majority of young women relinquishing babies for adoption gave their unmarried status as their reason for doing so.[27] These young, unwed mothers had no power to advocate for themselves, and state systems took advantage of this. By the 1950s, birth mothers were almost entirely shut out from accessing any information about their babies through adoption agencies.[28] This became the policy and practice of most adoptions across the nation through the late 1970s.

A second fundamental shift was that medical advances in the decades leading up to World War II radically transformed people's understanding of fertility. Before this time, doctors could not conclusively determine what obstructed conception. But now, for the first time, doctors and scientists understood reproductive endocrinology, and nonsurgical procedures were devised to understand the details of ovarian function. These medical advances quickly led to the new, booming industry of fertility treatments and clinics.[29] As private fertility practices sprouted up across the country, women were running the gauntlet of tests and procedures to determine if they could have their own biological children. And when a definitive *no* came from their doctor, they could walk out of the fertility clinic and down the street to the local adoption agency. Couples armed with knowledge were navigating these new systems in order to create the families they wanted. Conspicuously, this fertility research and testing focused almost exclusively on women's reproductive abilities, a practice that denies the reality we know today: in a third of all infertile couples, the problem lies in the man's fertility, one-third lies with a woman's fertility, and one-third cannot be identified.[30] In these postwar years, women were taking the full brunt of infertility shame and culpability. It was the expectation that they could and should become mothers; when they could not biologically bear children, the responsibility of that failure landed squarely in their laps. But regulated, private, discrete adoption agencies offered a solution to absolve them of their failure to conceive.

The third major shift in the post–World War II years was that demand for adoptable babies skyrocketed. And, unlike in the early 1900s, now couples specifically wanted babies instead of children. And they wanted not just one baby to adopt but multiple babies. Through the 1940s, the percentage of children adopted by families that already had one adopted child multiplied tenfold. By the 1950s, this number had doubled again.[31] In the early 1900s, families requesting children to adopt rarely specified a request for babies. Between 1930 and 1940, the percentage of families requesting babies instead of children to adopt doubled. By the 1970s, 98 percent of all adopting parents specifically requested newborns.[32] This transition in demand away from children and toward babies was reflective of a trending philosophy stating that nurture trumped nature when it came to childrearing. Infant adoptions promised the assimilability of the baby into the adopting family's norms and culture. Even if the baby was born to a poor, undereducated teenage girl, if it was adopted young enough by a highly educated, wealthy couple, there was assurance that that baby could shed its biological predispositions and blend seamlessly into an upper-middle-class lifestyle.

The pathology and stigmatization around adoption were not in the action of transferring a baby from birth mother to adopting parents but in acknowledging that this transaction had really happened, as had an illegitimate pregnancy. Those adoptees who found out they were adopted and sought answers from private adoption agencies were often labeled as aberrant and represented a failure of the adoption process. Carp provides this example in *Adoption Politics*: "In 1958, one CHSW [Children Home Society of Washington] adoption worker described an adult adoptee searching for his birth parents thus: 'the troubled adult was a pretty unhappy, disturbed person.'"[33]

This thinking speaks to the philosophical foundation of adoption that nurture supersedes nature in child development. If the child failed to assimilate to and fully embrace the adopted family culture, denying all connection to biological roots, or if they even publicly acknowledged that they were adopted, then that adoptee was considered troubled. Some states, including Oregon, which had amended its laws before World War II to allow adoptees access to original birth records, now worked to repeal those laws out of fear that troubled adopted adults would cause harm to their adoptive parents by accessing the truth about their births. In defense of the repeal, the legislative committee agreed that "ultimately the potential 'heartbreak' to adoptive parents outweighed the adopted person's 'curiosity.'"[34] The appeal passed unanimously.

For a long time, I subscribed to this anti-search mentality to a certain degree. Although I grew up knowing that I was adopted, for most of my childhood, I believed that only desperate adoptees would look for their birth families. In my mind, it signified some failure on the part of both the adoptee and the adopting family if an adopted child wanted to find his or her biological family. When I was young, I rationalized that because I felt loved and secure in my adoptive family, I did not *need* to do a search. I did not need replacements. And, more importantly, a search meant something was incomplete in me. A search meant acknowledging that the adoption transaction had really happened. A search meant reconnecting—or attempting to reconnect—to the biological line that had been severed in the adoption process.

Similarly, birth mothers who advocated for keeping their babies, especially during the latter half of the twentieth century when adoptable babies were growing exponentially in demand, were stigmatized for wanting to keep their babies. In a 1957 statement from the CWLA, adoption agencies were encouraged to educate unmarried pregnant women about the extreme challenges of raising a baby successfully "in our culture without damage to the child or herself."[35] And those unmarried women who chose to keep their babies were labeled immature, selfish, and unsuited for motherhood. If these women could not become pregnant in an acceptable fashion, they were discouraged from even trying to mother in an acceptable manner. In this post–World War II adoption market, Black birth mothers were treated decisively differently from white birth mothers. Black birth mothers were much less likely to be encouraged to relinquish their babies, even when the CWLA began accepting babies of color in the 1950s. This was because, as sociologist and adoption researcher Katarina Wegar writes, "Black women and their babies were not valued as market commodities."[36]

The evolution of these adoption policies speaks to cultural assumptions about women and their expected roles in motherhood and the ways the intersections of race and class impact a woman's and a mother's value in society—both birth mothers and adoptive mothers. Women who did not mother correctly, namely poor unwed mothers, were shamed. Women who could not or chose not to conceive children naturally were also susceptible to public shame. And, in a vicious twist, the adoptive mothers were actually shielded from any possible connection to birth mothers, thus protected from the shame and public embarrassment the birth mothers—and the original birth certificate itself—could reveal about their perceived inadequacy as women. Women on both sides of this adoption equation were forced to live a lie, as was the adopted child.

In 1975, the year I was born, there was a significant decrease in the availability of babies, particularly healthy white babies, for adoption. This was the culmination of the 1960s sexual revolution coupled with increased access to birth control. Young women were having sex out of wedlock but now had the power to choose to not get pregnant. In 1973, the United States Supreme Court legalized abortion on the federal level with its watershed ruling in *Roe v. Wade*. Women who did get pregnant could now access safe and legal abortions. At this same time, Black social workers effectively organized to denounce transracial adoption. The civil rights and Black Power movements of the 1960s and 1970s inspired communities of color in all areas of work to fight for racial justice. Advocates for babies and children of color saw the growing trend of transracial adoption as cultural genocide and a blatant devaluing of families and communities of color. Between 1972 and 1975, transracial adoptions fell by 39 percent, with only 831 in 1975.[37] Yet the demand for white babies persisted at the same rate it had through the 1950s.

By 1975, some adoption agencies simply stopped accepting requests for healthy white infants, and social workers were informing prospective adopters that they would likely wait three to five years for a healthy baby.[38] Because of this high demand, case workers and other mediators in the adoption process began experimenting with allowing birth mothers to choose who they wanted to adopt their babies. This experimental policy allowed my birth mother to create restrictive requirements for my adoption, requiring graduate degrees and musical abilities on the part of my adoptive parents.

In the decades after World War II, demand for adoptable babies hit such a frenzy that social workers and adoption agents crafted and embraced a philosophy that not only justified but demanded the forced relinquishment of newborns, particularly from unwed white mothers. This was an about-face from the decades-earlier policy of keeping "natural" families together. The focus now was targeted specifically at unwed mothers, who were deemed unworthy of mothering and therefore made child separation necessary. Part of this philosophy involved pathologizing unwed mothers as being mentally ill. A researcher working with the CWLA in 1955 described unwed birth mothers as "not bad, but rather . . . sick. . . . Not only is one attempting to help the unmarried mother develop more mature methods of solving her problems than through her solution of getting pregnant, but one also is usually able to help the unmarried mother give up her baby for adoption."[39] As this statement implies, the second part of this philosophy was the *necessity* of relinquishing babies instead of supporting birth mothers in keeping their babies. Illegitimate pregnancies were being treated as illegal pregnancies.[40]

A birth mother chronicled in Karen Wilson-Buterbaugh's book *The Baby Scoop Era: Unwed Mothers, Infant Adoption, Forced Surrender* provided this testimony of her experience in a maternity home for unwed mothers during this time:

My clothes were taken away, my name was changed and I was not able to connect with the outside world. I compare my stay there to anyone who is abducted by a cult. I was brainwashed with propaganda of how sinful I was. I was treated like a second-class citizen who deserved to be treated as such for my sins and given tasks to do that no one nine months pregnant should be allowed to do, such as working in a laundry where the temperature exceeded 100 degrees. All of this was referred to as my punishment. The nuns at the home made reference to my unworthiness and to how grateful I should be to them for saving me. The social worker who visited me several times could handle my unwillingness to surrender the baby to CC [Catholic Charities]. My precious baby girl was never referred to as my baby because in the mind of the social worker I could never be a fit mother; perhaps someday, if I could be, I would have a baby of my own. But not this baby. This baby would go to people who were capable of being a real mother and father. After all, it was reiterated to me over and over again that I had nothing to offer my child. However, a married couple had plenty to offer my baby.[41]

The deceitful duplicity of this philosophy of punishing illegitimate pregnancies through the forced relinquishment of babies was that it completely denied the larger social context that was pressing upon young pregnant women during this time, namely a lack of access to highly demanded safe and effective birth control, compounded by a sexual revolution, and the lack of supportive prenatal care, health care, welfare benefits, and community support in general.[42]

Multiple forces, including a shortage of desirable, adoptable babies and advocacy work questioning the legitimacy and integrity of sealed adoption records and the forced relinquishment of newborns, were putting pressure on state agencies, social workers, and other players in adoption politics to change the way things were being done. The deeper questions that these forces were challenging people to think about were, Who is the adoption for? Whose well-being is of the highest priority and why?

During this heyday of private adoptions, those facilitating the transactions often encouraged adopting parents to never disclose to their children that they were not biologically related to their family. Hundreds of thousands of Americans were born, lived, and died never knowing that they were adopted, that their birth was a lie, that the blood coursing through their veins was not the same as that of their parents or siblings. But by the late 1970s, movements around the country to unseal adoption records were gaining traction. More and more adoptees began looking for their biological families and questioning the system.

My sister and I were adopted into a family that held a specific set of values and expectations. From a very early age, my sister refused to abide by any of them. She simply didn't fit this box of how to be in the familial world that my parents built for us. As we grew up and Rachel developed the persona of outsider, rebel, and freak, she both embraced this identity with a sense of rebellious pride and suffered dearly—physically, mentally, and emotionally—because she always lived on the outside, isolated, without a family to claim as her own.

For years, my parents kept a greeting card posted on the refrigerator that was referred to as Rachel's card. The picture on the card showed a black and white cat sitting on its hind legs with a puzzled look on its face. The cat is surrounded by a waddle of penguins on an iceberg. The caption below reads, "Bob always had a sneaking suspicion he was adopted." Despite the superficial humor of the card, in reality, it cut at a deep and painful truth that she didn't fit in. Rachel didn't look like the rest of the family. If her adoption had been orchestrated by the Cradle, she would have been identified as a bad match, with her bright blond hair and steely blue eyes, which stood in stark contrast to everyone else's brown hair and dark eyes. Rachel stood out. There was a mismatch in the constructed family, and she knew that, felt that, more than all of us. That was the secret truth in the adoption experience: the match, even when manufactured to look natural, is always in some way incongruent. The decades-long policies and practices that intentionally silenced the transfer of babies from one family to the next and shrouded the transaction in secrecy functioned like a cancer that is still felt by adopted people, even when we know we are adopted.

When I was in high school, I started really wondering about my adoption and my birth family. For the first time, I started asking questions. One day, my mother took down a box from a high back shelf in the utility room behind our kitchen and pulled out an old, large, rusted plastic safety pin. She explained that it had been the pin on the cloth diaper I was wearing when they picked me up from the hospital to adopt me. That's it. That was the only relic I had in my life from the time before I was adopted. That safety pin was the only object that connected me to my birth and my birth mother. That's it. There's no paper trail. No pictures. No names. Not even the name of an adoption agency. The whole transaction was so cagey that nothing remains except a safety pin. Sometimes even now, I wonder if I really was born, because there is zero evidence of it happening. Even my birth certificate is fake. But I have to have been born, because I am here.

I have about two hundred pictures from each of my daughter's births. We have hospital baby blankets, snippets of hair, ultrasound images, tiny newborn footprints on paper, hospital documents including newborn Apgar scores, birth announcements, and videos. I documented the hell out of their births. And this data, all this evidence, is my way of saying to my daughters, "You were born, I was there, and it matters. You matter. And you are meant to be here."

2

Assimilation

My older sister, Rachel, and I both have tattoos. For Rachel, tattoos expressed her resistance to assimilation into our adopted family. Humans from all parts of the globe have been inking their bodies for thousands of years; the earliest evidence of human tattooing goes back over five thousand years. These physical markers often symbolize one's status within a community. But they almost always signify a relationship with family, community, spirits, and earth. My sister's collection of bold and colorful tattoos represented her defiance and refusal to assimilate in that the tattoos directly contradicted our parents' Judeo-Christian cultural beliefs of what was civilized, acceptable, and right. This rebellion made our inked bodies extra dangerous and powerful in what they meant to us within our family community.

Being adopted requires a certain level of assimilation. All children, whether adopted or raised by their biological family, are forced to adapt to the rules and norms of the family culture. And every family has its unique way of being together and expectations regarding behavior, work, dress, relationships, education, and other practices. For the most part, kids, especially younger children, must get with the normative program of their homes and families. But for many adopted children, even at a young age, there can be a painful rub of discomfort with the adopted family culture, especially when it runs counter to their innate aspirations and identities.

As Sharon Kaplan Roszia and Allison Davis Maxon explain in *Seven Core Issues in Adoption*, "As a way of defending against further rejection, adoptees may work very hard to blend in, not complain, be grateful, not ask for what they need and please others at the expense of their own needs." This was me. I worked so hard to blend in, to be a part of a family whose binds and threads often felt uncomfortable and even, at times, distressing. Roszia and Maxon go on to write, "At the other extreme, adoptees may be angry, defensive and alone, or act as bullies so they can hurt others before they are hurt. They may exhibit destructive behaviors in order to maintain emotional distance from others or defend against creating dependency to avoid further traumatic loss, rejection and pain."[1] And this was Rachel. She always stood apart. As a young child, she stood apart physically and visually, and I often felt envious of this distinction and separateness, this uniqueness. As we grew older, her behavior, her clothing choices, her music choices, her food choices, her choice in boyfriends all amplified her separateness from our adoptive family culture.

Rachel's rebellion started small, like regular teenage stuff. She hung out at the bowling alley with the "bad" kids from school. She stole our mom's credit card. And then, one night, she was returned home by two police officers. She had been picked up, with several other high school kids, for underage drinking and loitering on public property. Several times before then, the police had left her in our driveway, never taking the time to actually ring the doorbell and talk to our parents. Of course, when they did, she took off the minute the cops pulled away. So by the time the police brought her to the door, it was not her first run-in with the cops. After this, after lots of trouble at school and more items stolen from home, Rachel was sent to a teen behavioral rehabilitation center. Years later, Rachel would argue emphatically that she was not an alcoholic or drug addict when she was first sent away. She believed she was just sent away because our parents couldn't control her. They didn't understand her.

When Rachel entered this first behavioral and addiction rehabilitation program, I was in ninth grade, trying to make my way through the gauntlet of high school. And I was doing this at the same high school she had left to enter rehab. Everybody at the high school knew that my older sister was in rehab. Trying to establish myself and my reputation separately from her was daunting. Teachers would pull me aside at the beginning of a new class and let me know that they knew my older sister and hoped I would follow a different path. Externally, this further engrained in me this near life-or-death desire to be good, to do good, and to assimilate to familial expectations, in contrast to the path my sister was following. But at the same time, these comments destroyed me. I loved my older sister. I had spent my childhood deliberately following her footsteps, feeling carried by her and deeply admiring her. Our new divergent paths as teenagers broke my heart. I hated myself for straying from her, for embracing this road of assimilation and the embodiment of an authority pleaser. At the same time, I was furious at her for choosing the path she was now on. She was no longer innocently acting defiant and pridefully independent but was now actively trying to light her path on fire along with anyone who dared to cross it.

At the end of my freshman year of high school, our parents made me attend a graduation gathering at Rachel's rehab center. This was a time when families were supposed to reconnect with their newly improved, sober, "fixed" teenager. It was one of the most uncomfortable experiences of my life. It was clear that Rachel did not want to be there, and she *really* did not want us there. After the horrifying event, several adults, family members of other teens in the program, came up to me and complimented me on my outfit, my demeanor, my hair. I had been identified as a rehab "inmate's" visiting young sibling. What they were really saying to me with those superficial compliments was, "Good for you for not being messed up like your older sister. You must be the good kid. Thank goodness your parents have you."

This mantra of being the good kid would follow me, repeated inside and outside my head, for years and years. And I bought the message thoroughly. I bought it because I thought if I embodied this position as the good child, we could avoid more horrible rehab programs, more miserable family therapy sessions, more embarrassing school expulsions. I also bought it because deep down, I wanted to prove to my parents that adopting me wasn't a mistake. They had gotten a good baby, one worthy of their love and attention. My ability to assimilate felt like a matter of life and death.

For a long time, I saw my sister's defiance as courageous independence. But it wasn't until after her death years later that I realized that part of it was rooted in the pain of being an outsider, of not having a family community that she could willingly and naturally meld to. And her tattoos became her armor against the painful rejection she felt deep in her core. Adopted children experience attachment and familial assimilation very differently than do children raised by their biological families. And this difference is even further exacerbated in transracial and transnational adoptions. As Lene Myong and Mons Bissenbakker write in their article on attachment in transnational adoptions, "For adopters and others with an investment in supporting transnational adoption, the concept of attachment extends a promise to secure adoptees' feelings of kinship and security within the intimate space of the adoptive family. For the adoptee, however, the notion of attachment-as-love organizes a narrative logic that places them between pathologisation and the demand for affective assimilation."[2] In this context, "children's assertion of agency is constructed as a problem."[3] Failure on the part of the adoptee to assimilate to the adopting family's cultures and norms is interpreted as, literally, pathological. Susan Harness, a survivor of assimilating Indian adoption policies and a member of the Confederated Salish and Kootenai Tribes, connects to the danger of this self-agency when she writes in her memoir *Bitterroot: A Salish Memoir of Transracial Adoption*, "I am isolated, an island in an angry white sea. Survival means silence; otherwise I know the anger will turn on me."[4]

People and institutions that have shaped adoption policy over the past century have a keen awareness of the power of assimilation in "successful" adoption projects. The welding of assimilation and adoption was most devastatingly practiced by the US government in its treatment of Indigenous babies and children in the 1960s and 1970s. In the mid-twentieth century, when adoption was becoming more prolific and institutionalized throughout the country, the US government decisively altered its policy toward Indigenous communities. Assimilation through adoption would become the guiding philosophy of this new US Indian policy with the creation of the Indian Adoption Project (IAP) in 1958. The project was directly and unabashedly a scientific experiment aimed at proving the effectiveness of assimilating Indigenous youth into dominant white culture through adoption. This was the US government's new solution to the "Indian problem," and this time, it would happen in the home rather than in boarding schools.

For centuries the US government has harnessed the power of assimilating others into an acceptable American identity to control people and land. In the late nineteenth and early twentieth centuries, this assimilation approach was done in government-run Indian boarding schools across the United States. This education policy contrasted with the previous policies of war and forced removal—both of which culminated in a near genocide of Indigenous peoples across the nation. The policy focused instead on assimilating Indigenous peoples through the dissolution of tribal reservation communities, individual land allotment, and

Indigenous socialization into the culture of private property. Reformers and policymakers saw the combination of land allotment and government-run Indian education as the way to "save" Indigenous peoples from exploitation and extermination and to assimilate Indians into white, so-called civilized society. Education, particularly in off-reservation, government-run boarding schools for Indigenous youth, would for decades serve as the assimilating tool, the vessel through which Indigenous youth would be washed clean of their Indigenous language, traditions, and spiritual beliefs and reformed in the classroom to become like whites in all aspects, including dress, food, work, faith, and language.

By 1931, 29 percent of Indigenous school-aged children were in government boarding schools.[5] Yet this was also a period in which the Bureau of Indian Affairs (BIA) was under political and economic strain, partially in response to the Great Depression and the fallout of the 1928 publication of *The Problem of Indian Administration*, a study led by Lewis Meriam and commonly known as the Meriam Report. Its goal was to identify problems within the BIA and offer solutions. The report's assessment of off-reservation BIA Indian schools felt "obliged to say frankly and unequivocally that the provisions for the care of Indian children in boarding schools are grossly inadequate."[6] The report's scathing review of BIA boarding schools highlighted as serious problems inadequate food and medical care of students, hiring and retention of poorly qualified educators, the uniform course of study, and, notably, the outdated vocational education program.[7] Its publication and circulation would signify the beginning of the end of BIA Indian education. As US government Indian schools lost federal funding and public support and began to close, the government had to find new ways to assimilate Indigenous youth into dominant white cultural identities. Its gaze turned toward Indigenous homes and began forging a federal assimilation-through-adoption policy.

The compounding social and economic devastation of government-run Indian education and allotment-era government policies stripped Indigenous communities of both land and economic autonomy. This, coupled with the fallout of the Great Depression, left Indigenous communities in the post–World War II years in extreme hardship. Generations of child removal and institutionalized education of Indigenous children in the BIA's boarding schools had contributed to the devastation of Indigenous communities and families. Multiple generations of Indigenous youth had lost their native cultures and languages and had been stripped of their rights to be raised within their ancestral communities, to be nurtured and loved by extended family networks.[8] By the mid-twentieth century, Indigenous communities had the lowest incomes and life expectancies and the highest rates of unemployment and suicide nationally. Infant mortality was three times higher among Indigenous communities than in the general population and even higher in some regions of the country.[9] Indigenous communities were in crisis.

In 1958, the BIA joined with the CWLA to begin the Indian Adoption Project in an effort to "rescue" Indigenous children from the poverty and destitution of Indian country, particularly "in the context of the rise in unwed [Indigenous] mothers who did not have the resources to care for their children."[10] Run by Arnold Lyslo, a former BIA employee, the IAP "placed Indian children in non-Indian homes and conducted research with the intention of showing the placement of minority children in nonminority homes was beneficial to children."[11] This new assimilation-through-adoption project, similar to earlier adoption projects, targeted young, unwed poor mothers as the culprits for all the problems that plagued Indian country. Welfare authorities and government officials really saw the Indian problem as the *Indian mother* problem. As social worker Stella Hostbjor noted in 1961, "Most of the Indian unmarried mothers we have known have had emotional problems which played a part in their illegitimate pregnancies, and that their behavior served a purpose for them."[12] Largely because of white cultural perceptions of marriage and family structure, Indigenous mothers were perceived as psychologically unstable and unfit to mother properly. Indigenous marital and communal childrearing practices were considered illegitimate and even devious. In an ironic twist, in the 1950s, Indigenous mothers were criticized by welfare officials for having sent their children to government-run Indian boarding schools and using these schools and other government resources as safety nets.[13] Indigenous mothers were deemed failures even when they acquiesced to assimilationist practices. Under these duplicitous and bigoted assumptions, the solution, as posited by the IAP, was to have white women raise Indigenous babies.

When the IAP officially began in 1958, director Arnold Lyslo initiated a process in which Indigenous babies and small children would be intentionally sent to non-Indian homes outside their states of origin. This interstate adoption model initially helped cultivate the project because non-Native communities in the Northeast and mid-Atlantic, where babies were being sent, were less prejudiced against Indigenous peoples. The mid-Atlantic region was also where the highest transracial adoption demands were.[14] The formation of the IAP coincided with a national boom in demand for adoptable babies in the post–World War II years.[15] There was a growing trend among middle-class white families to adopt babies of color. Hundreds of would-be parents began writing letters to the BIA specifically requesting to adopt Indigenous babies. Lyslo capitalized on this demand by focusing on adoption transactions geographically. This meant moving babies and small children far away from their birth communities. The interstate model also worked much like the earlier Indian boarding school model in that distance from the home culture was thought to facilitate assimilation into white culture. Indigenous children were raised hundreds, if not thousands, of miles away from their reservation communities, cut off from cultural, historical, and linguistic influences.

The program, as a social scientific project mapping the successful assimilation of Indigenous children, was funded by the Elizabeth McCormick Memorial Fund of Chicago and tracked the progress of assimilation in ninety-eight adopting families over a five-year period. The results of the project were published by David Fanshel in 1972 under the title *Far from the Reservation: The Transracial Adoption of American Indian Children.* The stated purpose of Fanshel's study was to learn more about Indian parents who wished to relinquish their children, the outcomes of Indian children's adoption, and "any significant cultural factors of the Indian unmarried mothers [compared] with the non-Indian unmarried mothers [and] how they plan for themselves and their children."[16] Although the project goals included concern for and interest in Indigenous communities, in reality, the project methods focused exclusively on the experiences of adoptive white families and their impact on their adopted Indigenous children. The personal experiences of Indigenous birth mothers and broader Indigenous communities were not remotely accounted for in the study.[17]

During the IAP program, 395 Indigenous children would be placed in white homes. But the program's influence was far-reaching. In 1965 alone, private and state adoption agencies across the United States placed 696 Indigenous children up for adoption; of these, 584 were placed with white families.[18] By the time the final IAP report was published in 1967, twenty-six states had established systems of adopting out Indigenous babies, and more than five thousand families in that year alone requested to adopt an Indigenous baby. In the conclusion of this final report, program director Lyslo quipped, "One can no longer say that the Indian Child is a 'forgotten child.'"[19]

In its blind ambition to assimilate Indigenous children through adoption, the IAP ignored not only the experiences of Indigenous birth mothers and Indigenous communities but also the experiences of the adopted children themselves. In 1974, Lee Cook, an Ojibwe social worker and president of the National Congress of American Indians, testified on Indian child welfare in hearings before the US Senate Subcommittee on Indian Affairs: "I think that the BIA and the state welfare workers have been carrying on like at Auschwitz."[20] Cook had an intimate connection to the plight of Indigenous children who were adopted out to non-Native families. His mother had died shortly after he was born, and his father had died when he was a young child. Like many Indigenous children, Cook was raised by a web of extended family, including grandparents, aunties, uncles, and cousins. He treasured his childhood, immersed in tribal culture and family community strengthened by ancestral knowledge. Conversely, Cook's close childhood friend, who was also orphaned, was shuttled into the off-reservation foster care system. Cook explains, "Our lives have never been parallel since. I went to prep school, he wound up in Redwing State School. I went to college, and he went to reformatory. I went to graduate school, and he wound up in Stillwater State Prison."[21] Cook saw his connection to his birth community as a foundational asset to his life trajectory. This asset was taken from his childhood friend, and Cook understood the devastating cost of this loss, equating it to genocide.

Lee Cook's tireless advocacy for Indigenous youth, along with the incredible work of many other Indigenous social welfare advocates, would eventually lead to the passage of the Indian Child Welfare Act (ICWA) in 1978. With the passage of the ICWA, tribal courts, not states, now had the authority to protect Indigenous children and stop the unwarranted removal of children from their homes, families, and communities.

Some of the most influential activists fighting to end the IAP were Indigenous mothers who witnessed firsthand the literal forced removal of babies and children from their birth families and communities. A group of women from the Devil's Lake Sioux

Tribe organized a Mothers' Delegation, hosting press conferences and lobbying efforts in New York and Washington, DC, in 1968. The Mothers' Delegation was a rallying cry for national attention to the atrocities of the IAP. The Association on American Indian Affairs (AAIA) allied with women of the Devil's Lake Sioux congregation and many other grassroots groups to gather data on "child snatching." Their data revealed that of the 1,100 Devil's Lake Sioux Indians under the age of twenty-one, 25 percent had been separated from their birth families.[22] By 1973, one in every nine Indigenous children was living outside his or her birth family or community nationwide.[23]

Even though the IAP formally ended in 1967, systems of child separation impacted Indigenous communities for decades. Through their diligence and perseverance, Indigenous advocates and activists pulled back the façade of "child and community welfare" that was the public-facing story of the IAP. Underneath was the reality of community trauma through assimilation. These activists' data collection and testimonies revealed hundreds of horrific cases of Indigenous mothers being forcibly coerced to relinquish their babies. The program had an abusive pattern of pulling children from their home communities, in many cases in direct opposition to both the child's and the community's requests, and placing children in off-reservation and out-of-state foster and adoption homes.

In the concluding report of the IAP, David Fanshel clearly describes Indigenous communities as continuing to struggle despite the project: "Reservations were still isolated, containing the 'worst pockets of poverty,' marked by high infant mortality, low health care, and worse housing than city slums."[24] In her in-depth critique as a researcher and survivor of the IAP, Susan Harness aptly points out that the public-facing initial intention of the project was to support reservation communities through the adoption of Indigenous children. In reality, the project's outcomes reflected only the continued trauma and alienation of reservation communities. In taking babies and children out of Indigenous communities to "tackle poverty and save those communities," the organizers and proponents of the IAP inadvertently revealed their true normative assumptions about Indigenous motherhood and family community. Indigenous communities and mothers were never considered valuable or capable of raising their own. And the outcomes of the project revealed its duplicitous intentions. Indigenous communities suffered even more because of the project, revealing that the welfare, health, and sustainability of Indigenous mothers and Indigenous family communities were never the focus of the project.

In the 1960s, during the height of the IAP, another devastating program began to affect Indigenous women's lives and reservation communities across the United States, revealing the pervasive distrust government agencies had of Indigenous mothers. Between 1960 and 1980, an estimated 25 percent of Indigenous women between the ages of fifteen and forty-four were sterilized by the Indian Health Service (IHS), a division of the US government's Department of Health, Education, and Welfare (HEW).[25] The sterilizations often occurred without the women's consent, without the necessary information, and under flagrantly false pretenses. Dr. Connie Pinkerton-Uri, a Choctaw and Cherokee physician who worked in Los Angeles in the early 1970s, was the first to report horrific cases of forced and misinformed sterilizations. One of her patients, who had been sterilized by the IHS, came to Pinkerton-Uri requesting a "womb transplant." The patient had been told by the IHS physician who gave her a hysterectomy that she could reverse the sterilization procedure whenever she wished with the nonexistent transplant. Dr. Pinkerton-Uri had to inform the patient that she had been lied to and would never get pregnant again. Dr. Pinkerton-Uri would discover that this devastating case was only the tip of the iceberg. One IHS clinic in Claremore, Oklahoma, had sterilized one in every four Indigenous women who came through the clinic to give birth. In total, more than forty-one thousand Indigenous women were sterilized by IHS doctors in the 1960s and 1970s.[26]

The forced removal of Indigenous babies and children through the IAP, followed by the coercive sterilization agenda of the IHS, exposed the devastating narrative propagated about Indigenous families, particularly Indigenous women. They were considered unworthy of mothering. As historian Margaret Jacobs succinctly writes, "Disturbingly, most bureaucrats by the late 1950s rarely imagined a solution to the care of Indian children that involved strengthening Indian families and keeping Indian children within their homes. Most government officials deemed Indian families inherently and irreparably unfit."[27] Indigenous forms of child-rearing themselves represented a failure to assimilate to the dominant white family structure and parenting practices. Aleta Brownlee, one of the lead staff of the BIA Welfare Branch, responsible for the "readjustment program" of assimilation through boarding schools to the start of the IAP outlined the key principles of the desirable American family life, which the US government felt could best raise children:

1. The father works and supports his family to the best of his ability.
2. The mother cares for her home and her children, keeping them clean, well-fed, properly clothed, and happy.
3. Both parents maintain for themselves and establish for the family standards of morality.
4. The parents are concerned for the education and the future of their children.[28]

This image of the ideal American family, as depicted by Brownlee in 1958, was the standard to which Indigenous families were held in order to determine their ability to care for and raise children.

The traditional family structure of one working father and one stay-at-home mother with multiple children living together as a fixed unit in one living space ran counter in many ways to the diverse, multigenerational, and community-focused childrearing methods common in many Indigenous communities. Métis scholar Kim Anderson draws on Cree and Métis metaphors of concentric circles to describe Indigenous conceptions of mothering and community childrearing:

> In this worldview, children are at the centre of the community. The elders sit next to the children, as it is their job to teach the spiritual, social and cultural lifeways of the nation. The women sit next to the elders and the men sit on the outside [of the circle]. For these points they perform their respective economic and social roles, as protectors and providers of the two most important circles in our community. Everyone in the community has a connection to the children, and everyone has an obligation to work for their well-being.[29]

In this worldview, children raised by extended families, including grandparents, aunts, uncles, and cousins, sometimes living in multiple homes, were cared for by the multiple layers of a community.

But in the eyes of BIA and IAP social workers, this childcare model was perceived as inadequate, even abusive. The IAP actively worked to demonize Indigenous communities in order to fill the demand for adoptable babies by creating several stock images of the "forgotten Indian child," the unmarried, negligent Indian mother, the deadbeat Indian father, and the deviant Indian family.[30] These images were filtered through mass media in newspapers and magazines, including the hugely popular magazine *Good Housekeeping*.[31] If a young Indigenous woman became pregnant and she did not fit the model of being legally married and having her own home and the financial ability to be a stay-at-home mother, with the *perceived* ability to focus her energy solely on the education and well-being of her child, she became a target of government social workers. That child needed to be "saved" from his or her Indigenous community, and that mother needed to be sterilized.

The US government's social health care and welfare approaches to saving Indigenous communities ignored the strengths that these communities possessed, including multigenerational community care that highly valued children and saw them as the backbone of tribal survival and sustainability.[32] As Lee Cook emphasized in his powerful testimony to the US Senate Subcommittee on Indian Affairs, addressing Indian children's welfare in 1974, to lose children was literally a form of genocide for tribal communities. Chuck Hoskin Jr., chief of the Cherokee Nation, drew a similar parallel in 2020 between the sterilization program of the IHS and the Jewish Holocaust when he explained, "A good portion of a generation of Native Americans was wiped out as a result of the sterilizations, which is a familiar theme in American history. But it takes on a particularly sinister connotation when we're talking about sterilizations by the government. There's another government in world history that did that too."[33]

One impetus for the IHS's sterilization program was the perceived threat of increased birth rates in Indian country. According to the 1970 census, the average Indian woman bore 3.79 children, whereas the median for all groups was 1.79.[34] By 1980, birth rates for Indigenous women dropped to 1.99, a startling decline in just ten years.

Women's autonomy over fertility and community practices in childrearing have been integral to many Indigenous communities for millennia. As Cheyenne tribal judge Marie Sanchez affirmed, "The Native American woman is the carrier of our nation."[35] The power of fertility connects directly to many Indigenous women's leadership positions within their tribal communities. To take away women's autonomy over their fertility and connection to their children is a direct threat to the sustainability of the community. Plummeting birth rates in Indian country were a direct threat to Indigenous peoples. At a 1979 conference on birth control, Katsi Cook of the Mohawk Nation declared that "women are the base of the generations. Our reproductive power is sacred to us."[36] In her testimony against the IHS sterilization program, Dr. Pinkerton-Uri said she didn't believe that the US government was directly, intentionally trying to exterminate American Indians through the program. Rather, the policy evolved through "the warped thinking of doctors who think the solution to poverty is not to allow people to be born."[37] This same mentality extended into IAP policy in that its solution to poverty in Indian country was not allowing poor Indigenous families to raise their children.

The philosophy of fighting poverty through sterilization and adoption projects was not exclusive to the United States. This same mentality would be echoed in state programs across the globe, particularly in the 1980s and 1990s when international adoption became a booming multimillion-dollar industry. One of the most prolific and horrific anti-poverty programs during this time was orchestrated by Chilean fascist leader Augusto Pinochet. Under the Pinochet government, thousands of babies, particularly Indigenous Mapuche babies, were taken from their families and put on the international adoption market. This "anti-poverty" program, like others in Korea, Vietnam, Russia, and parts of Central and South America, would fill a pipeline of babies being adopted into American and European homes at the end of the twentieth century.

The collective impact in the United States of forced adoption and sterilization policies on Indigenous communities that lost children, women who lost autonomy over their fertility, and Indigenous peoples forcibly segregated from their birth communities would have ripple effects for decades to come. Dr. Connie Pinkerton-Uri, along with Mary Ann Bear Comes Out and Cheyenne tribal judge Marie Sanchez, collected testimony and data from hundreds of women who were duped into sterilization by the IHS. Their data demonstrated that the sterilizations trauma-tized not only the women but also their extended families and tribal communities. The women they surveyed poststerilization dealt with higher rates of "marital problems, alcoholism, drug abuse, psychological difficulties, shame and guilt."[38] The loss of reproductive autonomy had a devastating impact on entire Indig-enous communities.

Deborah Thibeault and Michael S. Spencer connect histori-cal trauma, as revealed by research, directly to the impacts of the IAP. They report that assimilation attempts through the IAP "created significant trauma, such as emotional, physical, and sexual abuse and loss of identity."[39] One of the educational aims of the Indigenous activists who worked to end the IAP and fought tirelessly for the passage of the ICWA in 1978 was to educate the American public on the significance of tribal sov-ereignty.[40] This meant shifting the dominant thinking that Indigenous people were simply a different, monolithic race, a mentality that fostered transracial adoption. Many white fami-lies seeking to adopt Indigenous babies believed that by being raised in white culture, the children could fluidly become white by simply assimilating into the dominant culture. Tribal sovereignty meant acknowledging the different, diverse tribal nations and communities, each with vastly different languages, cultures, tradi-tions, and histories. The impact of the IAP was that children would not grow up Standing Rock Sioux, Diné, Yakima, or Chippewa. Personal memoirs and narratives written and shared by survivors of the IAP speak to the cost of these adoption transactions that segregated children from their tribal cultures, communities, and histories and the deep impact this had on their identities.

Susan Harness synthesizes the consequences of adoption: "Adoption, by the very act itself, is defined by tragedy; death, the inability to be a parent (as in the case of my birth mother) and, in my case, the inability to be a whole and complete child."[41] Har-ness was born in 1959 on the Flathead Indian Reservation and adopted out at the age of two when she was removed from her home by a social worker who deemed her familial living conditions "negligent."[42] In her memoir, Harness writes about her experience being raised by white parents in Montana, and then finding her way back to her ancestral roots later in life. Her raw, powerful memoir details her childhood being raised in an adopted family that she describes as "volatile and fragile."[43] Her adoptive father was an alcoholic, and her adoptive mother suffered from severe depression. Harness sums up her upbringing:

> My family of alcoholism and mental illness was not much different than a lot of families in America. And to be fair, I did get a lot of success, and access to social and cultural capitals I wouldn't have had (I probably would not have graduated from HS with my birth family—no one did), from being raised within that family, but I as an individual, paid a high price for those successes, because of my Indian-ness in the social world.[44]

In the descriptions of her childhood in a predominantly white community in Billings, Montana, Harness speaks to the experience of being loved by her adoptive parents. But that love came from who they wanted her to be, not who she was or where she came from. Her father referred to Indigenous peoples, her ancestors, as "god-damn-crazy-drunken-war-whoops."[45] In her family's childhood garden, her father had a little cement statue of a picturesque blond-haired, blue-eyed toddler girl, which he doted on and meticulously repainted every spring. This cement statue would come to represent the blond-haired, blue-eyed girl he had always wanted, a role Harness could never fill with her dark skin and hair. Harness's sorrow emanated from her painful position in a liminal space, as neither white enough nor Indian enough.

Anecia Treikoff (Sugpiaq), another survivor of assimilating Indian adoption policies, speaks to this liminal space of being not white enough and simultaneously cut off from her Indigenous culture and history. In her powerful testimony, Treikoff also connects the impacts of the US government's assimilation-through-education policy to the IAP:

> Because my mother was taken into the dominator's boarding school and made vulnerable in the world by separating her from her family and tribe, she acquiesced to the stinging, convincing words to let me go to the white man's church-people with the hopes they would find a wonderful family for me. I am indebted [to] my adoptive parents who did choose to parent me and raise me in the best way they knew how. But I hence forth must accept that I am a guest among my tribe. Anyway, my lack of tribal knowledge and family history must make me seem like some sort of imbecile in a place where the connected members are at home.[46]

The loss of a feeling of home, felt in one's core, is fundamental to many adoptees' experiences. And the inner tension of either willingly or unwillingly resisting assimilation into one's adopted family culture only exacerbates this liminal space of homelessness.

In her qualitative research on transracial adoption, Susan Harness concludes that assimilation through adoption is, in essence, both futile and detrimental. Through extensive data collection and interviews with adoptees, many of whom were survivors of the IAP, Harness's goal is to understand "why the American Indian adoptee who has been placed in a Euro-American home has such difficulty 'fitting in' or 'belonging.'"[47] Unlike previous psychological and sociological research on adoption outcomes that almost unanimously target unfit birth mothers as the culprits for the future failures of their adopted-out biological children, Harness's research exposes the detrimental effects of invisible societal structures, experienced after the adoption transaction, that prevent or significantly hinder adoptees' belonging to either their birth communities or their adopted communities. These invisible yet highly consequential cultural and societal forces that continually push on adoptees through their lives, *after* they have been adopted out, "explain why a sense of belonging was so elusive, why American Indian adoptees did not feel comfortable in either ethnic identity."[48] In her memoir, Harness describes in explicit detail the long-term microlevel impacts of these invisible societal structures that leave transracial adoptees in a perpetual position as outsiders:

> Interaction is culturally defined. I've spent my life learning it, using it, perfecting it. I can translate people's facial expressions, body language, subject matter, with amazing clarity. I've spent a lifetime doing it. In a white world. But here on the rez, I know nothing. I can't read these faces; I can't read their body language. I can't interpret their responses or lack of responses. I can't read between the lines of what is being said because I've never been taught how to. Those within this culture don't see the ways of communicating as unique; they just *are*.[49]

Cultural assimilation through adoption has the power to situate adopted people in isolating spaces of belonging nowhere.

When I was a sophomore in high school, Rachel was sent off to an out-of-state rehabilitation program in Provo, Utah. And I decided I needed to leave too. Life at home felt unbearable. I applied to several college-prep boarding schools, all 2,500 miles away, on the other side of the country. And in the fall of my junior year of high school, I was heading off to a boarding school in New Hampshire. Our two schools couldn't be more different. Rachel's school, in the desolate Utah desert, focused on "fixing" dysfunctional, problematic teenagers. My school, in the White Mountains of New Hampshire, focused on paving strategic paths to Ivy League colleges. But both schools offered us something we needed: an opportunity to get out and start over. Yet there was a fundamental distinction in how we both got out. Rachel's exit from home, to a teen rehabilitation and behavioral modification program, was shrouded in shame. My exit, to a distinguished New England college-prep school, was held up as a badge of honor, a symbol of acceptability and success. My school symbolized successful assimilation. Rachel's symbolized an epic failure to assimilate.

The juxtaposition of Rachel's and my experiences in school echoes Lee Cook's comparison with his childhood friend who was forced into the foster care system off the reservation and away from his birth community. Similar to Cook's account, I succeeded in high school, then college, then graduate school, as my sister went in and out of rehabilitation programs and jail and struggled to stay employed and sober. One significant difference between my story and Cook's is that he was raised by his birth community. I was not. I was raised in an adoptive family culture, severed from my birth family and any ties to my blood ancestors. Where I succeeded and my sister failed was in my acquiescence to assimilating into my adopted family's cultural expectations.

One outlet of resistance to this assimilation, for both of us, was our tattoos. Rachel encouraged me to get my first tattoo. This was her not-so-subtle way of getting me on the anti-assimilation bandwagon. For this first tattoo, I chose a small flower on the inside of my ankle. It was a quiet, malleable form of resistance that I could hide with pants and socks when I felt the need to safely assimilate into my adoptive family's cultural expectations. My second tattoo was very different. The second time, I got a tattoo to mark being embraced by a community rather than my resistance and refutation to a community and family I did not choose. When I got this second tattoo, I was on the other side of the planet from my family, on a journey to define myself on my own terms with a crew tied together by choice on a physical and metaphorical journey.

After graduating college, I signed on as paying crew on a traditionally rigged sailing ship to sail around the world for two years, learning the skills of an able-bodied seaman and accruing sea time so that I could sit for a US Coast Guard captain's license. On this slow journey sailing around the globe, our crew would spend a significant amount of time traversing Polynesia, living and working with local families and communities and learning about Polynesian culture on a grassroots level. We would come into ports of call in Tahiti, the Cook Islands, Samoa, and Tonga, to resupply, do repair work, and explore. Because we were a working ship with a trading and educational program, we linked up with local communities in the smaller ports we stopped in. We were able to participate with local communities in schools, houses of worship, and family homes and to learn from local communities in a meaningful way things that tourists who fly into major airports and head straight for the luxury resorts don't experience. And, for the first time in my life, I saw and experienced the art of tattooing as a practice wholly antithetical to shameful rebellion, but rather as a highly revered practice of honoring and connecting to one's culture, ancestors, and the power of the natural world.

By the time our ship entered Polynesian waters, many of the crew had embraced the culture's traditional practices of tattooing. As we were assigned work leave from the ship and were given time off in rotation to venture onto these island paradises, my crewmates began returning from their work leave with traditional tattoos on their arms and legs. Some of the crew connected with local tattoo artists on the island atoll of Bora Bora who practiced the time-honored art of tattooing with a boar's tooth. A tradition emerged among the ship's crew: every time a crew member returned with a tattoo, he or she would be publicly celebrated and asked to share the tattoo and its meaning. These tattoos became a symbol of our crew's ritual, marking our collective survival and resilience in the challenges we faced as we sailed around the globe.

Encouraged by this rite of passage my shipmates and I were going through, I decided to get a tattoo while we were at port on Morea, in Tahiti. When I sat down for this marking, I asked the artist to select a symbol to fit around my first tattoo, the flower. After an hour of quietly drilling with a modern tattoo gun, he looked up and shared what he was working on. He had styled a fishhook, curved around the flower and shaped with the bold, dark markings of a cresting wave, carved along the edges of the hook. The fishhook, or *makau* in Marquesan and Polynesian culture, symbolizes a connection between the wearer and the ocean. It is a sacred representation of safe passage over water.

In Polynesian culture, tattooing is a practice of socially patterned wrapping of the body. The tattoo is both a shield protecting one's mana and an insignia confirming one's place in relation to her community. According to Marquesan cosmology, the world consists of *po* and *ao*. These two spaces are not dichotomous but rather balancing and intertwined. Po is the world of dark and night and the realm of the gods. Ao, space of light and day, is the domain of humans. Here on earth, in the domain of humans, there are people, objects, and places representing po and ao. Those that belong to po, the realm of the gods, are said to possess *mana*. Mana is the divine power affiliated with the gods, expressed in procreativity, fertility, power, and war.[50] The *makau* is a connection, like the Marquesan cross, between po and ao.

Wrapping my skin in the makau became a way for me to protect my mana and define myself on my terms. I see my makau tattoo as a representation of mana that I did not have in my adopted family culture: "The body is our basis to identify ourselves as different from others and thus is also the medium with which we relate ourselves to others. We form personal and social identities and establish social relationships through the body. Furthermore, the manipulation of the body by, for example, tattooing can be considered an active practice with which people engage in self-identification and positioning in their relation-ships with others."[51]

My makau became a symbol of assimilation into a new family, my chosen ship family. This was the first time in my life when I felt I belonged. We were a group of outsiders who collectively fit together. A handsome, kind, honest, and unconditionally loving young man was part of this motley crew. We fell in love before the ship had left the dock in Canada at the start of the voyage, even though we didn't put our hearts out on our sleeves and admit our love for each other until we were deep in the Polynesian Triangle, in the Cook Islands. Four years later, I married that amazing man, with over twenty of our ship's crew in attendance as we said our marriage vows. Through our marriage, this ship truly became family.

3

Birth

My two daughters are the only people I have ever known to whom I am biologically related. They are my true anchors, tethering me to my past and my future. Their lives and my experiences as their mother, especially the experiences of bringing them into the world, have peeled back a false sense of safety and security I had lived with throughout my life.

I met my first anchor, my first baby girl, on February 9, 2010. I had been in labor for nearly forty hours. My husband and I had made a birth plan. We had taken a birthing course. We knew how we wanted it to go. I was going to have a beautiful, natural birth in the big birthing tub in our delivery room. It was going to be wonderful, easy, and peaceful. My husband ended up napping in the tub. We never filled it up with water. My daughter's long, thin umbilical cord was wrapped twice around her neck. She was trying to get out but was hanging herself in the process.

In the thirty-ninth hour of labor, I was told I had to give up my natural birth plan, and the anesthesiologist started me on Pitocin. Shortly after that, my baby girl's heart rate started to plummet. I was lying on the hospital bed, restricted by cords and tubes, distracted, and panicked by the tightening of my huge belly and the dull ache of my back and legs. I watched the heart rate monitor next to the bed like a hawk. My heart was racing. I wasn't sleeping. I was on the biggest adrenaline rush of my life. I hardly blinked as I tracked my baby's heart rate up and down, up and down. And I knew something was wrong. After what felt like five hours but was probably more like thirty minutes, a nurse walked swiftly into the room and said it was time to go to the operating room. I just said, "Okay, let's go."

This began the scariest twenty minutes of my life. I was wheeled into the operating room, briskly wiped down, slid onto the operating table, and pumped full of drugs to counteract the Pitocin. I vomited continuously into an outstretched bag that a nurse held next to my head by the operating table. I alternately retched and scanned the room in a state of horror at the look of tension and concern on the face of every single person surrounding me on the operating table. As the doctor began cutting open my belly, I could literally feel her hands pulling and stretching my abdomen in order to reach inside of me and pull my baby's head, which was stuck in the birth canal. At this point, someone woke my husband, who was snoring in the bone-dry birthing tub in the birthing suite. He was briskly told to put on scrubs and come into the operating room.

As the doctor and nurses were in the process of pulling me open to get their hands around my baby's slippery little body, my husband, bleary-eyed and half-dressed in scrubs, shuffled into the operating room to see the gaping incision on my abdomen. He sat down quickly so that he wouldn't pass out, crack his head on the cold linoleum floor, and become the next patient. My husband and I were both nearing a state of shock. But the minute our baby girl was freed from the birth canal and I heard the nurse wiping down her little, pink body say that she was healthy, breathing, and beautiful, we were both okay. We were great.

In a split second, I went from horrible and terrified to more elated than I had ever felt. By now, I was a physical mess, covered in my own vomit, feces, and blood and shaking violently and uncontrollably. I was shaking so hard I kept banging into the side-walls of the hospital gurney they had heaved my massive, messy body onto from the operating table. I was shaking so hard I could barely hold onto my baby when they put her in my arms. But the smell, the mess, and the chaos didn't even register for me. For the first time in my life, I was meeting my child, my blood, my people. Holding my daughter in my weak, shaky arms was electrifying. Having her little body next to mine immediately wiped out all the physical trauma my body had gone through over the past forty hours of labor and emergency surgery. My husband and I couldn't stop touching her and looking at her. Holding my baby or watching my husband hold her gave me the greatest sense of peace and calm I have ever known. She was the drug that cured me of all the pain I had suffered.

I don't take for granted for a moment the privilege of growing my daughters in my belly, of feeling them kick and struggle and fight for life. And then to hold them and nurse them at birth, to feel their tiny, fleshy, pristine bodies against mine. To know that they grew inside me, came out of me, yet are now totally independent of me, is nothing short of a miracle. When I see my daughter twist her hair because she is nervous, just as I do, or when I see in pictures that my daughter is the spitting image of me at the age of four, I take none of this for granted. This biological connection is magic to me; it is a privilege of which I am in per-petual awe. I see a look come across one of their faces that I imme-diately recognize because it's my look; I relate to it and understand it. And even in moments when my daughters are driving me crazy, I see myself in them and recognize the privilege of witnessing that connection. I spent thirty-four years of my life feeling like a part of me was missing. The birth of my daughter woke me up to what I had been missing. I had grown adept at hiding my incon-gruity, isolation, and pain. Now, I felt wholly complete for the first time in my life.

When my first daughter was born, I knew in my body, as an indisputable truth, that my birth mother had suffered on the day she gave birth to me and left me at the hospital. I had been told my entire life that she had chosen to give me away, chosen a large hospital where she could relinquish me without holding me, so that she could be free to walk out the door and continue with her life as if nothing had happened. On the day I gave birth to my first baby, I knew that even if my adoption was her choice, it was not done easily. It was not done without immense suffering and trauma, and she did not walk out of that hospital to pick up her life as it was before.

In their research on the adoption experience, Sharon Roszia and Allison Maxon write at length about the significance of this prenatal bond formed between mother and baby: "Birth/first mothers have had a nine-month relationship with the baby that grew inside them. For most, this was a deeply intimate and bonding experience that is broken when the baby leaves."[1] I felt this connection, this bond, so deeply that it literally shook me to my core. Seeing and holding my baby for the first time after she was outside my body was like a public, open acknowledgment of this relationship we had been building together for nearly a year. It didn't start at her birth; it began months earlier. But the birth was so profound because that was when the outside world acknowledged it, could see it, could see us. It was a public validation that she and I had done something amazing and miraculous together as a team. My bond with her was intoxicating, and I felt that my life depended upon keeping her as close to me as possible to maintain that bond. Yet I also felt the deep pain of my own severed bond from when my birth mother let go of me. Losing a baby, even through a chosen relinquishment, is traumatic. Losing a baby through forced relinquishment is trauma compounded. As Roszia and Maxon write, "The traumas of losing a child, infertility and adverse childhood experiences are intergenerational issues. Trauma can change one's genetic code. This change has been proven by following African Americans, Native Americans and Holocaust survivors intergenerationally and is referenced as 'historical trauma.' Trauma leaves its mark on cultures, world views and physical well-being."[2]

The practice of assimilating children into American culture through adoption has become baked into our society as something that is both gallant and patriotic. This is a cultural practice that necessitates a baby being taken from a traumatized birth mother, who in many cases is suffering under multiple layers of duress. In the mid-twentieth century, Harry and Bertha Holt were instrumental in crafting the template for transnational adoption. The movement they set in motion—transferring babies and children from predominantly poor, war-torn, and disenfranchised communities into US and Western European homes—became a template for transnational adoption. This template depended heavily on the coercive, forced relinquishment of babies and small children from mothers and extended communities that did not want to lose their children.

One evening in 1954, when McCarthyism fever was just breaking in the United States and the aftershocks of the Korean War reverberated across the Pacific and the continental United States, Oregon farmer Harry Holt watched the film *Dead Men on Furlough*. The propaganda film, produced by World Vision, Inc., was intended to incite fear of a global Communist takeover and posit American evangelical reforms as an antidote to the evils of a spreading anti-Christian Communism. In the emotive opening of the film, narrator Bob Pierce describes Communist citizens as literally dead, soulless "animals, ready to die and kill, lie or cheat" in the name of Communism.[3]

Greatly moved by the film, and particularly the plight of Korean children born to Korean mothers and American GIs, Harry Holt traveled to war-torn South Korea to adopt and "save" these so-called GI babies from the evil influence of Communist North Korea. While Harry was in South Korea, his wife, Bertha, lobbied Congress to pass a bill making transnational adoption legal. Through a special act of Congress in 1955, the Bill for Relief of Certain War Orphans—known as the Holt Bill—was signed into law, officially making the international transfer of babies and children in refugee status federally legal.[4] Harry Holt returned to his family farm in Creswell, Oregon, with eight biracial, Korean-born children. He immediately received national attention as an American savior.[5] Over the next decade, Harry and Bertha's evangelical, transnational adoption operation would transport thousands of Korean children across the Pacific and into white Christian homes across the United States.

The Holt organization's unorthodox and highly unregulated program caught the attention of the USCB and the CWLA, both working actively to regulate adoption procedures and squelch the rampant and abusive practices that had defined American adoption in the early twentieth century. But Harry and Bertha Holt demonstrated an impressive ability to commandeer public political support for their transnational adoption practices. Through their close friendship with then Oregon senator Richard L. Neuberger, the Holts, under the extension of the Refugee Relief Act, acquired immediate and permanent visas for the children they were shipping over from South Korea. The USCB and CWLA had minimal jurisdiction over transnational practices and were swamped by their regulatory responsibilities with stateside adoption.[6] And so, for the next decade, the Holts ran a largely unregulated, highly prolific, and pioneering transnational adoption market.

Using a provision of this act [Refugee Relief Act] permitting Americans to adopt orphans by proxy—adoptions completed abroad by a third party without the parents' presence—the Holts rapidly processed adoptions and sent planeloads of children to US families. They bypassed the long-established social welfare procedures that ensured domestic orphans' protection and used the refugee measures to avoid racially restrictive immigration quotas. Although the proxy process was legal, social-work organizations believed that the Holts' interpretation of the law endangered children, offering them limited recourse from risky placements.[7]

Within just years of the Holts' adoption of eight Korean children, they were inundated with letters from hopeful adopters begging for access to adoptable Korean babies. Their campaign was written about in *Life* magazine and *Reader's Digest*, and the Holts were becoming household names across the United States.[8] Although the Holts' initial mission was to place Korean babies and children only in Christian homes, by 1964, demand from Christian families had waned. To continue the program, Harry and Bertha decided to expand access to non-Christian families, but they did so with great reluctance. In 1994, Bertha Holt wrote that through her career adopting out children, she prayed daily that "every child we process will become a Christian."[9]

Proselytizing and American assimilation were components of the Holts' strategy in these pioneering years of transnational adoption and enabled them to win the support of many powerful political leaders in Washington, DC, and across the country. When the Holts initially devised their plan to save biracial Korean children after the Korean War, anti-Asian immigrant sentiment was strong in American culture. Before World War II, anti-Asian international policy, shaped by the Chinese Exclusion Act of 1882 and the Immigration Act of 1924 (Johnson-Reed Act), which excluded all Asian immigrants on the basis of race, had infiltrated American culture. Bigoted fears of uncivilized Asian immigrants who were coming to steal jobs and wreck the American way of life persisted even after the passage of the Immigration and Nationality Act of 1952 (McCarran-Walter Act), which liberalized immigration law and allowed Asian immigrants to become US citizens.[10]

But there were still strict quotas on Asian immigration, and they presented a barrier to the Holts' plan—as did the racism white families would face when they brought home Asian babies. The Holt strategy of presenting their adoption project under the guise of child redemption through American Christian assimilation enabled the American public to see these adopted children as their own and not a foreign threat. The angle of religious and cultural assimilation through adoption was reinforced by the Refugee Relief Act—which President Eisenhower urged Congress to pass in 1953—enabling adoption programs to circumvent immigration quotas. Eisenhower wrote in his letter to Congress that refugees, children included, were "look[ing] to the free world for haven."[11] The American rhetoric of humanitarian exceptionalism, coupled with the promise of assimilation of young Asian children managed by white, Christian parents, would start to turn the tide in favor of transnational adoption.

The Holt adoption program's strategy of adoption by proxy, which would come to define transnational adoption until 1961, allowed organizations like the Holts' to operate under refugee relief status and streamline the transfer of children across the globe by eliminating the need for American adoptive parents to make the exhausting trip to a faraway, foreign, and wholly unfamiliar place. These parents gave Holt power of attorney to navigate Korean law on their behalf; conversely, Holt was given legal guardianship of the adopted children, allowing him to send the children out of their home countries without supervision from a birth parent or adoptive parent.[12] Adoption by proxy also strategically allowed for a nearly insurmountable geopolitical segregation between birth mothers, birth family communities, and the babies and children being shuttled out across the globe. It also "provided the added benefit of not having to contend with the

foreign parents or their inferior culture according to applica-
tions."[13] American adoptive parents wouldn't have to risk coming into even regional contact with birth mothers or communities.
And the South Korean orphanage set up and managed by the
Holt adoption program could intentionally orchestrate strategies
for forced separation between children and birth mothers.

The Korean language had no word for adoption, and many
birth mothers who relinquished their babies and small children
at the doorstep of the Holt orphanage did not understand that
this was a permanent separation, that they would never again have
access to or see their child.[14] And as with later strategies employed
by orphanage directors in Vietnam, the Holts specifically targeted
highly vulnerable, impoverished, often single mothers of biracial
children. To contend with other adoption organizations vying
for Korean babies, the Holt adoption program in the late 1950s
began air-dropping leaflets in rural farming communities outside
Seoul. The leaflets advertised that if women relinquished their
babies at the Holt orphanage, the babies would be saved by God
and promised a better life in the United States. Much was lost in
translation, and, as with the tragedies of Operation Baby Lift
two decades later, many Korean birth mothers did not know that
this relinquishment meant forever.

In 1966, a decade into the Holt adoption program, Bertha Holt
was named "American Mother of the Year," an honor bestowed
upon her by the Johnson administration, in collaboration with
American Mothers, Inc., a national committee founded in 1933
and born out of Eleanor Roosevelt's creation of the federal obser-
vance of Mother's Day. The committee's mission continues to
be to "help dependent mothers and needy children."[15] The criteria for eligibility for Mother of the Year include a woman who
"embodies traits highly regarded in mothers and displays the ability to strengthen family relationships through maternal energy."[16]
The Holts successfully forged a lasting bond between American
exceptionalism and transnational adoption. In naming Bertha

Holt American Mother of the Year just a decade into the Holts' transnational adoption project, the committee and the government were codifying the embodiment of the ideal American mother as a white, Christian woman who was saving babies and children from the evil savagery of illegitimate, impoverished, war-torn birth mothers. The Holts' form letter sent out to adopting parents included this statement: "We ask all of you who are Christians to pray to God that He will give us the wisdom and the strength and the power to deliver his little children from the cold and misery and darkness of Korea into the warmth and love of your homes."[17] By choosing international adoption, American women could save these babies from the "darkness of Korea," and Bertha Holt was their new champion.

Two hundred thousand babies were adopted from South Korea and placed in homes in the United States between 1954 and 2020.[18] In 1975, the Holt organization was responsible for evacuating 409 babies and children out of Saigon. The evangelical organization started by Harry and Bertha Holt, now called Holt International, is a multimillion-dollar industry and the premier transnational adoption organization in the United States, choreographing the transnational adoption of children to the United States from South Korea, Vietnam, Thailand, India, Guatemala, Romania, China, Mongolia, the Philippines, Uganda, Haiti, and Cambodia. Adopting through Holt International costs between $24,000 and $52,000 per child.[19]

By 1975, the year I was born and relinquished by my birth mother, the national perception of adoption was shifting dramatically away from a silent, secret, shameful narrative to one of heroism and patriotism. The nation was in its last year of another weary and highly problematic two-decades-long war, this time in Vietnam. One of the most dramatic moments occurred at the very end of the war, three months before I was born. Operation Babylift was the mass evacuation of thousands of infants and young children out of South Vietnam as Saigon fell to the North Vietnamese. It was coordinated between the United States and several other countries, including Australia and Canada. In April 1975, four dozen large-carrier flights flew more than 3,300 babies and children out of Vietnam, 80 percent of them coming to the United States for adoption. The confluence of high demand for babies to adopt and low supply of adoptable infants, combined with the circumstances around the end of this bloody, tragic war, would all feed an ethos in America that adopting foreign babies was both a patriotic duty and a great humanitarian act. Operation Babylift triggered a new wave of adoptions in the United States; international adoptions would become a booming trend for decades.

The Vietnam War spanned five US presidential administrations, from Eisenhower through Ford. Vietnamese babies were born into the war; they grew up and had their own children during this brutal war, never knowing what it was like to live in peacetime.[20] Twenty years after it began, the end finally came into view in March 1975. North Vietnamese troops attacked Ban Me Thuot in the Central Highlands of South Vietnam and began their push toward the South Vietnamese capital of Saigon. Highway 7, a narrow, rugged mountain pass in the Central Highlands, became instantly filled with half a million South Vietnamese refugees desperately flooding toward the southern and coastal regions. The last few weeks of the war were marked with sheer desperation and brutality—families were ripped apart in the chaos as people tried to escape and survive.

War creates endless victims, but one of its cruelest and most consistent victimizations affects children. According to South Vietnamese government statistics, the nation had 879,000 orphans by 1975. They included children whose parents were dead or could not raise them. By this point at the end of the war, 134 orphanages were operating in South Vietnam. These orphanages cared for roughly 20,000 orphans. They operated on minimal resources and lacked money and basic supplies. Death rates in these orphanages ranged from high to extraordinarily high. But the vast majority of South Vietnamese orphans, the remaining 860,000 parentless children, were cared for by relatives or neighbors. An informal yet highly interconnected and effective fostering network evolved in Vietnamese culture to care for these youngest victims of war. Nearly 20 percent of all South Vietnamese families had an orphan living with them by the end of the war.[21]

The philosophy and dogma that drove the most prominent and influential leaders of South Vietnamese orphanages, who were not Vietnamese themselves but rather white women, dictated that the Vietnamese government could not protect the lives of their children and should abdicate this responsibility to volunteers who could protect the children and send them away to have better lives. Rosemary Taylor, a white woman from Australia with no formal training in adoption practice or policy and who rose through the ranks as a volunteer, led four orphanages in Saigon and became one of the most influential players in the international adoptions out of Vietnam and the outcome of Operation Baby Lift. Taylor was an unrelenting advocate of international adoption, making it her life's work to get as many Vietnamese babies out of the country as possible. Taylor would write in her memoir years later,

> Nothing in my previous experience or reading had prepared me for this. I was coming into contact with hundreds of newborn babies with no identity and no prospects. There were healthy and handicapped babies; the fully Vietnamese and the mixed-race, the legitimate and the illegitimate. Poverty, illegitimacy, birth defects, and the fact that the children were never "wanted" should account for most of the abandonments, but there were also a few orphaned through the death of the mother, or abandoned by a wealthier family because of an inauspicious birthdate.[22]

Like many orphanage leaders in South Vietnam, Taylor firmly believed that all the babies who came into her care were unwanted

and that the best outcome for them was to be adopted out overseas, far away from the war, from their native country and cultural homeland.

But not all babies and young children who moved through
these orphanages were unwanted or even orphaned. And as the
war neared its desperate and chaotic end, in the weeks leading
up to Operation Babylift, the lines between which children were
actually orphaned and which had families but needed temporary
care became even more blurred.[23] Many of the babies and children
moving through these South Vietnamese orphanages were *con lai*,
meaning they had Vietnamese mothers and American fathers.
This mixed-race, half-American identity largely fueled the US
government's support for the evacuation project. These babies
had American blood pulsing through their veins, and the US government felt a special obligation to save them. The circumstances of these con lai babies' birth and the relationships between
their Vietnamese mothers and American soldier fathers were
complex and varied widely. Some of these mothers were poor, and
many were widows with children they were struggling to raise.
Many of these single mothers worked on military bases as laun-
derers, cooks, and translators. For some of them, a liaison with
an American soldier offered camaraderie, financial security, or
love. But by early spring of 1975, these mothers, now with an
additional child to feed, were once again struggling alone.[24] By
1975, most American military personnel had been called back to
the United States.

Con lai babies and children stood out on the streets of Saigon
and Danang with their afros or blond hair, blue eyes, and fair or
black skin. Their existence was a daily reminder of America's contested presence in Vietnam. According to street gossip in communities throughout South Vietnam, the North Vietnamese soldiers
hated con lai children and planned to kill them when they took
the South: "They would slit open the belly of a con lai, pull out
the liver and eat it."[25] These rumors terrified mothers like Kim,

who had con lai children. Kim was married with multiple children. Her husband, a drafted soldier in the South Vietnamese army, had disappeared, and she was left to fend for herself and three children. She got a job working in the laundry of a US Navy hospital near Danang. An American officer on the base treated her with kindness, building a house for her, providing her with money to help feed her children, and taking the family out to eat at a restaurant on Sundays. Kim repaid him with sex. Her body was the valued resource she had. Kim became pregnant, and the American officer left Vietnam before their daughter, Hiep, was born. Like many US soldiers, he would never meet or care for his child.

As the North Vietnamese army pressed farther into the South in the winter of 1975, Kim became desperate with fear that Hiep would be slaughtered because she was of mixed race, her blue eyes a symbol of the enemy. In March 1975, Kim took Hiep to Danang to an orphanage called Me Quoc Te, whose name means "International Mother." Me Quoc Te was known for sending babies and children overseas for adoption. Hiep was only seven years old; Kim believed she could make this trip with Hiep and stay connected to her, even through the adoption process. After giving the American orphanage officials Hiep's information, including her birth certificate, Kim begged the officials to let her go with Hiep. In less than an hour, the officials had started taking babies and children down to Saigon to be flown out of the country for adoption. The official told Kim it was too late; she could not come. Hiep and Kim wept. Hiep begged to stay with her mother, but Kim grew stern and said to Hiep, "If you stay here, the Communists will kill you and waste your life. You're going. You can go to school. I gave birth to you and now I'm letting you go because if you stay here, you will die." Hiep was forced out of her mother's arms, shuttled onto a bus full of small children, and driven to the airport to be flown away.[26]

Kim's story is one of thousands more from con lai mothers who were forced, in sheer desperation, to make unbearable choices for children they deeply loved. And for thousands of these mothers, their pregnancies were not the result of a loving or even willing relationship but instead the result of rape. "Throughout history, women's bodies have constituted an important part of the spoils of war," and the Vietnam War was no exception.[27] Because there has never been a war crimes tribunal established to officially document and prosecute American military service members for rape in the Vietnam conflict, the actual number is unknown. But abundant personal and witness testimony collected by independent organizations over the years makes these war crimes well-documented. The testimonies of Vietnamese women who were brutally raped by American GIs have intentionally been silenced in a deliberate effort by the US government, the military, and the media to "restore the comfortable myth of American exceptionalism," especially in the face of the highly problematic and epic failure in foreign-war policy that was the Vietnam War.[28] The deliberate action of silencing the experiences of Vietnamese women who were brutalized by American soldiers and then abandoned to care for their con lai babies also facilitated further dehumanization of these birth mothers. If adoptive parents across the Pacific didn't have to know that the babies and children they were welcoming into their homes were the result of rape by American soldiers, they could better justify their patriotic role in saving the child through adoption.

Years after the end of the Vietnam War, a website called Vietnambabylift.org published a "Looking for" page that served as a bulletin board for birth families and adoptees trying to reconnect.[29] Thousands of posts from Vietnamese mothers and other family members, desperately searching for children who had been sent away in those last frenetic months of the war, demonstrate that Taylor's claim that these babies were "unwanted from the start" was not a clear assessment of the situation.[30] Powerful forces outside Vietnam made decisions that would forever change the lives of these babies and young children—decisions largely based on assumptions and void of the voices and experiences of Vietnamese communities. At the core of these decisions were judgments about who would make a better mother and parent. Through the two decades of the war and for years after, the vast majority of South Vietnamese orphans were cared for by relatives or neighbors in Vietnam. Their worth and value as acceptable guardians of children were negated or completely ignored.

The story of Operation Babylift is not told from the perspective of con lai mothers. Our historical understanding of the event and the wave of transnational adoptions that would proliferate in the United States for decades would be told and understood from the perspective of American policymakers and predominantly white American families adopting foreign babies. An April 1975 article in *Time* magazine described Operation Babylift thus: "Not since the return of the prisoners of war two years ago [has] there been a news story out of Vietnam with which the average American could so readily identify, one in which individuals seemed able to atone, even in the most tentative way, for the collective sins of governments."[31] Operation Babylift represented an atonement for past sins, American sins. Saving these babies wasn't just about saving babies. It was a way for America to feel better about itself, to feel good and clean and moral in the face of a brutal war.

The feel-good story that frequently stimulates adoption policy, especially international adoption policy, is rooted in a belief that a baby is being saved from an illegitimate, unworthy mother and community. The baby is plucked from evil and despair and placed in the arms of hope and opportunity. But this story is almost always told from the side of the savior: those people, organizations, and governments that represent hope and opportunity. It's a very one-sided story. And it's incredibly effective at reinforcing this uplifting narrative around adoption. Two months after Operation Babylift, I was born and adopted. I was born into a nation desperate to heal from the war, and adoption was seen as a method of healing. But who was being saved through these adoptions?

The babies? The parents? The nation? All of these distinctions were blurred.

Operation Babylift centered transnational adoption as a force for good in a highly public and pervasive manner. The national success of this operation in the United States sheds light on how transnational adoption morphed from a short-term emergency refugee policy into an entrenched multibillion-dollar American industry. War-torn nations in distress, like Korea in the 1950s and Vietnam over the next two decades, provided fertile soil for a burgeoning new era of adoption as American demand for adoptable babies spiked and the market for available babies in the United States plummeted. The impetus for adoption practices in both war-torn regions of Asia was initially to save the multiracial babies of GI fathers and impoverished Korean and Vietnamese mothers from a life of "uncivilized" destitution in Asia. In the resulting policy and practice vacuum of transnational adoption in the 1950s and 1960s, black markets and systems of abuse, deceit, and outright child trafficking proliferated into the later twentieth century.

These transnational adoption projects also became a method employed by fascist leaders who saw transnational adoption as a vehicle through which they could maintain social control and pad their personal coffers. In South America in the 1970s and 1980s, "a critical relationship exist[ed] between child appropriations, 'irregular adoptive practices' and dictatorial regimes."[32] One of the most horrific examples of these practices developed in Chile between 1973 and 1990, under the fascist Pinochet regime. Pinochet's adoption policy intended to eliminate poverty through population control with the added benefit of financial gain on the part of many of those involved, as they profited from the growing international adoption market. A complex system involving nuns, doctors, lawyers, social workers, and international adoption agencies operated to secretively and efficiently funnel upward of twenty thousand babies and children out of Chile and into the

United States, Holland, Sweden, and Germany.[33] So successful was Pinochet's program that Chile ranked in the top six countries sending children for international adoption between 1980 and 1989.[34] According to Chile's own Court of Appeals, at least eight thousand of those adoptions were conducted under suspicious and abusive circumstances.

Pinochet's program specifically targeted poor, Indigenous Mapuche women. These women, already vulnerable to other socioeconomic and political forms of abuse, had almost no way to advocate for themselves and their babies. This made them prime targets and helped justify Pinochet's larger "anti-poverty" platform. Decreasing the number of poor people in the country, starting with Indigenous babies, would inadvertently increase the overall wealth of the nation. Practices involved cajoling young, single pregnant women to willingly give their babies up at birth. On a more vicious level, newborn babies were also directly stolen from mothers, in hospitals, with the help of nurses, doctors, and hospital staff.

Tyler Graf, later a Houston firefighter, was one such baby. Tyler was born in a hospital in Santiago, Chile, in 1983. His mother, Hilda Quezada Godoy, was an Indigenous Mapuche woman from rural Temuco. Tyler was born three months premature and had to spend the first weeks of life in a Santiago hospital's neonatal care unit. Hilda would travel back and forth, visiting her newborn in the hospital. One day when she arrived at the hospital, she was told her son had died, with no explanation. In reality, Tyler had been moved to an orphanage, his birth papers falsified, and then sold for adoption to an American couple in Minnesota who believed that his birth mother had willingly given him up because she was too poor to raise him.[35]

Tyler Graf and Hilda Godoy's horrific story is not singular or even unusual. Of the thousands of babies who were stolen from their mothers under the Pinochet anti-poverty program, it was common practice for midwives who worked for the clandestine project to tell grieving mothers that they could not hold or see their dead babies because they had already "been brought to the oven to cremate them."[36] In 1989, the United Nations Convention on the Rights of the Child (UNCRC) was ratified, declaring that in adoption, "Due regard shall be paid to the desirability of the continuity in a child's ethnic, religious, cultural and linguistic background."[37] This provision becomes challenging to adhere to when everything surrounding the adoption of the child and their birth family is a lie. And although the United States has signed the UNCRC, it is the only United Nations member state that has not ratified it.

International adoption into the United States almost tripled between 1989 and 2001, rising from seven thousand to over twenty thousand transactions a year.[38] The foundation of this project of bringing babies and small children into the United States—or, as Eisenhower put it, into the "free world for haven"—bolstered American exceptionalism by positing this picture of the American family as savior. But the image denied the reality of hundreds of thousands of birth mothers and communities that were preyed upon and then ignored to complete transactions. Their collective trauma of having their babies taken from them has left an indelible mark on the multibillion-dollar transnational adoption industry that flourishes today.

When I learned I was pregnant, it was one of the happiest days of my life. My husband and I had been trying for several years to conceive. After two years of trying to get pregnant, we finally decided to see a fertility doctor. I learned I had severe endometriosis and a large fibroid on my uterine wall, which drastically impeded my ability to conceive. I then spent multiple months on hormonal treatments to mitigate the endometriosis and shrink the fibroid. As a result of this medication, I would sweat profusely, and I was incredibly short-tempered and emotionally drained.

After enduring four months of this treatment, I went off the medication and we did a round of artificial insemination at the fertility clinic. I became pregnant on the first try. Pregnancy literally felt like the greatest accomplishment of my life. I had sailed around the world, but that was nothing compared to getting pregnant, which felt like the hardest thing, physically and emotionally, I had ever done. Conception did not come easy, and we were so incredibly grateful it had finally happened for us.

My pregnancy was such a joyous celebration, not just because I had overcome these physical obstacles but also because our community and larger society reinforced the idea that this pregnancy was valued, that I was a valued pregnant woman, that I was and would be a valued mother. I was valued because I had the acceptable identity to mother a child. I was a white, highly educated, middle-class, heterosexual, cisgender, married woman. I fit into this bubble of acceptability, and my new status as a mother added an additional layer of legitimacy to my life and my existence. As a woman, I was following the expected behavior. My baby would come into the world loved and valued.

Unlike mine, my birth mother's pregnancy thirty-four years earlier was not a celebration. The births of thousands of babies during the Korean and Vietnam wars and under the brutal Pinochet dictatorship were not celebrated. The mothers were not uplifted, celebrated, or valued, particularly by the adoption programs whose goal was to take their babies overseas. These pregnancies and the babies themselves were problems that had to be dealt with, and these birth mothers were left traumatized and ignored in the wake of losing their babies. My birth mother was single, she was young, she was a student, and her pregnancy was also a mistake. Her pregnancy was outside the box of acceptability. Adoption is traumatic. And when that adoption is not a choice, made deliberately and freely by the birth mother, the trauma can be unfathomable. Decades of adoption policy ignoring the experiences of birth mothers and the confluence of powerful forces that dictate who is valued as a mother and who is not perpetuate this trauma.

On our first night home from the hospital after our first daughter's birth, I remember sitting on the floor of the bedroom, holding my tiny baby and just weeping and weeping, my body shaking uncontrollably. It was a strange, out-of-body experience because I didn't fully understand at the time why I was crying. I had hormones, mixed with lots of drugs from my emergency C-section, still coursing through my body. My body and my emotions were a wreck. In addition to still aching from the procedure, I was now worn down from sleep deprivation. When my daughter was born, I felt like I was on the greatest high of my life. But now, two days into motherhood, I had plummeted. I hurt. I was exhausted. But mostly, I was absolutely terrified. My birth mother couldn't raise me; how the hell could I raise a baby? I suddenly felt like this journey I had just begun was too much, too big. But still, at that moment, I couldn't understand why I was just sitting there weeping while I held my baby, this miracle that I had waited so long for. She was healthy; I was healthy, for the most part. We had made it through that intense birth journey.

Years and hours of therapy later, I realized that I cried that night because, unlike my beautiful baby girl, who was held and loved and touched from the moment she left my body, I wasn't touched or held by my birth mother during those first two days of life. My birth mother had suffered through a long hard labor and then walked out of the hospital alone. Holding my baby daughter that night, I wept for me, and I wept for my birth mother. The birth of my own daughters woke me up to an immense feeling of compassion and grief for what my birth mother went through on the day I was born. I understand now that giving me up must have been the hardest thing she ever had to do. It took giving birth for me to realize this on a deep, unquestioning level. My birth was not a celebration. It was traumatic.

Although I do not have a mental, cognitive memory of my birth, I do have, for the first time, a deep emotional memory of it. Kapi'olani Laronal writes about the power of the gut and the womb to remember and find meaning:

> Indigenous resilience teaches us that the body, in alignment with the spirit of people and place, is a source of intelligence beyond our mental capacities to hold information. Meyer (2001) cites Kanahele, who identifies the "na'auao," the enlightened stomach: "It's a cosmic center point. It has to do with your ancestors coming together with you. It has to do with your spiritual being coming together, it has to do with our physical being." Kanahele's "cosmic center point" identifies the gut as an internal compass containing all ancestral and present-day memories without our physical, mental and heart-centered realms.[39]

When my gut and my uterus, my cosmic center, were torn open, out flowed those subconscious emotion-based memories of when I had slid out of my mother's womb thirty-four years earlier. I was there, conscious, alive—and so was she. We shared that memory even though it would be erased on paper and falsified on legal documents as having never happened as it did. For the first time, I remembered my birth, and it brought me to my knees as I held my baby, my birth mother's granddaughter.

4

Motherhood

Inadequate mothers (approximately 33 percent of all
mothers) constitute "just about the number one
problem in America."

> Marynia Farnham and Ferdinand Lundberg,
> *Modern Woman: The Lost Sex*, 1947

As an adopted child, when the inception of your life is defined by
mistake and ignominy, you find it challenging to redefine the
experience of fertility and motherhood on your own terms. I continue to struggle to define myself in addition to and beyond the
almost stifling restrictions of "mother." The idealized image of
who is a good, valued, and acceptable mother in American culture is restrictive, immutable, and so embedded in every facet of
our culture that we are almost unaware of these norms and societal forces that are constantly, relentlessly pushing on women.
Being born to a woman who was shamed for my conception, being
given away at birth, and then, years later, struggling with fertility has given me the ability to see the duplicity and inequity in
how our society opens its hearts and minds to mothers differentially. But it wasn't until I became a mother myself that I felt the
true force of being positioned in a lane of acceptable motherhood that I still struggle to navigate.

One month after my first daughter was born, I received an acceptance letter from the University of Washington's doctoral program in education history. Throughout my pregnancy, I had spent my time alternately lying on the couch eating burritos, studying for the GRE, and applying to graduate school. It was a surreal experience, vacillating between my physical body, which every day was changing into this out-of-control, unrecognizable, bloated ball, and my head, as I desperately tried to relearn polynomial functions, precalculus, and geometry so I didn't completely bomb the math portion of the GRE.

I sat for the GRE when I was seven months pregnant. I had to pee the entire time. I sweated through every layer of clothing I had on. My feet swelled up from sitting for so long that by the time the testing ended, I had a hard time standing up and had to hobble desperately to the bathroom, sweat dripping down my face as I was sure I was going to have an accident before I made it into the stall. I couldn't get out of that testing center fast enough, and I was certain my chances of getting a remotely acceptable score that would allow me to even be considered for the UW doctoral program were totally dashed. I drove home crying.

Five weeks after my daughter Maria was born, I received an acceptance letter to the doctoral program. I gave birth thinking that this next mountain I so desperately wanted to climb, pursuing a doctoral degree, was out of my reach. In its place lay a sweet, pink little creature who continuously pooped and ate and wanted nothing more than me holding her. She was my new adventure. But then that letter came, and that mountain reappeared through the fog like a beacon of hope. After my dumpster fire of a GRE, my friends and family had reassured me that motherhood would ease the disappointment. Countless people told me that once my little baby was in my arms, I would have a new purpose in life, and graduate school would fade in importance. When I read my acceptance letter, it was so clear to me how wrong everyone had been. I held my tiny newborn daughter in my arms while I read the acceptance letter. She lay staring peacefully at me with her big blue eyes. I looked at her, and at the letter, and without a doubt in my mind I told her I was going to get my PhD and climb that mountain.

I started the doctoral program in the fall of 2010, when my first baby girl was seven months old. Most of my classes were in the afternoon or evening, so I would leave my daughter at home with the babysitter for a few hours until my husband came home from work to relieve her. I would get home sometimes as late as ten o'clock. That first year of coursework was a blur. I would sit in lecture halls with eighty other students for three hours at a time, listening and taking notes, all the while my breasts leaked all over my desk. I would have to position my laptop delicately on the edge of the tiny foldout lecture-hall desk so that I could type without leaking milk onto the keyboard. I was so embarrassed in the beginning. I didn't look like the other doctoral candidates sitting in the classroom: everyone else looked so young and full of energy. Even though I was only thirty-five years old, I felt about fifty. I was constantly exhausted. After class, people would gather for drinks or food at an off-campus pub. I would rush to my car and drive home to nurse my baby. But as physically and socially uncomfortable as this time was, I loved it. I loved the mental distraction from parenting. I loved immersing myself in reading and writing about history, as opposed to worrying about my baby's growth chart and the consistency or color of her poop. I loved climbing into the car three afternoons a week and driving away from the house, knowing that for the next five hours, I was only responsible for myself.

Halfway through my first year of graduate school, I became pregnant with our second daughter, Victoria. This pregnancy was not planned. It was a surprise, like a flooded basement is a surprise. We were unprepared, but at the same time excited. It had taken three years of painful disappointment, laborious and anxious-ridden fertility doctor visits, and hundreds of hours of general anxiety before getting that first positive pregnancy test. And then, boom, here came the second one, effortlessly. We were blown away. My husband lost his job shortly after I found out I was pregnant. The compounding financial stress was almost debilitating. But the silver lining was that now my husband was home every day with our daughter, searching for jobs while she napped and taking her to our local zoo for afternoon walks and playtime while I dragged my once-again swollen pregnant body off to graduate school for class.

At the end of the first year of graduate school, I had to meet with my advisor, the professor who would, in many ways, determine my fate as a PhD candidate. She had the power and authority to sign off on every hurdle of my research and writing journey. I had to tell her I was pregnant and needed to take a quarter off to have my second baby. My advisor was a woman; I had that working in my favor. But she did not have children. She went through graduate school and years of teaching, researching, and publishing unencumbered by pregnancy or childcare. The afternoon I met with her to share my news, I waited and waited outside her office, once again nervously sweating through my clothes. When she finally opened her door and invited me in, I shuffled into her office, slumped into a chair, and looked down at my swollen feet, the tops of which were already starting to bubble out over the edges of my shoes. My poor feet were going to kill me for this second pregnancy.

When I opened my mouth and told my advisor I was pregnant and would need time off to have my second baby, her initial response was so unexpected that it wasn't until months later that I realized it was problematic. She asked, "Do you plan to have any more kids?" Why should it matter if I were going to have another baby? Did my ability to research, write, and teach correlate with the number of children I had? Perhaps indirectly, but so did my ability to pay for childcare. The university was committed to a policy that students should not be held back by their or their family's access to resources; the school worked tirelessly to create pathways of access and success for students living in poverty. So, what was different about the burden of having children, especially considering that I had the privilege of being able to afford childcare? Having children presents, especially for women, a certain level of burden, as does a lack of financial resources. But the mother status, with the unique burden it brings, is treated much differently by society. The burden of the child is seen as the *mother's* responsibility, and attention to other work is perceived as an irresponsible distraction. That child is her burden to carry, and it must be carried as her primary focus.

Pregnancy and childcare become obstacles for women not because women and mothers cannot work, create, build, design, and lead when they are pregnant and parenting. Rather, these obstacles emerge because of the restrictions, expectations, and limitations society puts on women as they carry their babies in their wombs and care for them after birth. We paradoxically expect both less and more from mothers. We expect less in their ability to think and function, particularly in roles not related to mothering. Yet we set an insanely high bar in the exclusive area of mothering. We shame pregnant women and mothers when they don't adhere to the narrow confines of acceptable mothering. While I was pregnant and nursing babies through my first two years of graduate school, I continually thought about my birth mother. She carried me in her womb while she, too, was in graduate school, studying to be a lawyer. But unlike me, she was told these two roles, mothering and law school, were incompatible, even with just one baby. Her family encouraged her to give me up when I was born because I would ruin her legal career. She was shamed not for pursuing a law degree as a woman, but for pursuing a law degree as a pregnant woman.

In a 2017 sociological study on national attitudes toward mothering, researchers found that despite wide variations in mothering experiences across different American cultures, races, and socioeconomic strata, the white, middle-class woman's experience with motherhood had become "the presumed norm and standard by which all mothering is judged." This white, middle-class norm defines ideal motherhood as "pronatalist," meaning that in order to mother at this standard, women must invest all of their time and material resources in their children. The study defines this standard of mothering as "hegemonic mothering."[1]

This image, of course, denies the economic realities that preclude millions of women from pouring an unending wealth of time and resources into their children. Mothering outside this image is seen as unique and deviant. Despite being statistical norms in American society, single mothers, immigrant mothers, and welfare mothers are labeled and judged as outliers and—most significantly—problematic. Further problematizing women who fail to mother in this hegemonic image, these deviant mothers are depicted as hyperfertile and sexually irresponsible for becoming mothers and then failing to measure up to the standard. Lastly, and equally destructive, this pronatalist, hegemonic image of good mothers also demonizes women who choose not to become mothers at all. In the hegemonic mothering image, all women can and should want to become mothers. This duplicity of both demonizing and celebrating women for their fertility, based on racial and economic identity, results in "social policies that discourage births among poor women and women of color, but promote births among white and middle-class women."[2]

Current legal practices regularly criminalize nonhegemonic mothering. Parental liability statutes, for example, are laws that impose liabilities on parents or guardians for the civil or criminal acts of their minor children. These statutes became standard across the United States in the early twentieth century as state and federal forces began regulating childcare and adoption practices and attempting new strategies for punishing "deviant" children. These early laws were so far-reaching and punitive that poor parents could be and were frequently criminally prosecuted for failing to provide a home above the poverty level.[3] These laws helped to justify the literal stealing of poor immigrant children out of their homes and placing them out for indentured servitude.

Parental liability statutes fell out of favor in the mid-twentieth century, in tandem with the civil rights movement, as more progressive policies around family care and engagement with social services took precedence. But, over the past thirty years, these statutes have made a shocking resurgence and are now actively enforced in almost all states. These modern statutes differ from the ones imposed a century ago in that they now hold parents strictly liable for children's illegal actions, as opposed to also issuing punishments for the children. This is reflective of modern social welfare policies that "attribute juvenile misconduct to improper parenting."[4] Recent legal research reveals that these archaic statutes, now meant to prohibit juvenile delinquency, specifically target Black and Latina single mothers. Legal scholars critical of these statutes draw a direct connection between the racist and misogynistic application of these statutes and societal conceptions of hegemonic mothering: "Parental liability statues perpetuate the idea that unwed Black mothers cannot be proper parents. For example, while society may view an unwed Black teenager's motherhood as 'illegitimate' or 'deviant,' the teenage mother may consider being a mother 'fulfilling' and a source of 'self-affirmation.' In addition, Black mothers may not address certain of their children's delinquent activities in an effort to maintain the family unit and open communication."[5] Parenting, and particularly mothering, has been and continues to be under the cultural, political, and legal microscope. The consequences of "deviant" mothering continue in severity and result in public shaming. And, at the extreme, in coerced sterilization.

Nefertiti Austin, a Black writer and adoptive parent, powerfully synthesizes the consequences of hegemonic mothering when she writes, "Mothering, in America, ten years ago and today equals white."[6] In *Motherhood So White: A Memoir of Race, Gender, and Parenting in America*, Austin critically unpacks the liminal space she exists in as an adopting Black mother who has to navigate mothering outside the norms of Black American society, where Black adoption means adopting within the blood family, and also outside the norms of white American society, which celebrates only white adopting parents. Austin was born in 1969, the love child of two young, passionate Black activists who were focused and dedicated to changing oppressive systems. Both were active in the Black Power movement in Los Angeles but were not ready to raise children. By the time Austin was nine years old, she and her young brother had been adopted by their maternal grandparents through the Black community practice of Black adoption. No papers were signed. The county was not involved. It was a community agreement between her parents and grandparents that Austin and her brother would now be raised by their grandparents.[7]

Black adoption meant that the roots and threads of Austin's cultural, familial, and ancestral connections were not severed. In Black adoption, birth documents are not falsified and sealed away. Austin was raised in a family where her image was reflected in the faces of her caregivers. She remained connected to her past. She knew her people. This also meant that she was not a stranger to her birth parents. She was raised by her grandmother, who deeply loved Austin's mother. Although there was deep sadness around her mother's struggles with addiction, there wasn't shame around where Austin came from. Six years before Austin and her brother went to live with their grandparents, the value of Black adoption and family preservation was demanded as a priority by the National Association of Black Social Workers (NABSW) at the National Association of Social Workers (NASW) Conference in 1972. Part of its declaration included the following statement: "The family is the basic unit of society; one's first, most pervasive and only consistent culturing life experience. Humans develop their sense of values, identity, self concept, attitudes and basic perspective within the family group. Black children in white homes are cut off from the healthy development of themselves as Black people, which development is the normal expectation and only true humanistic goal."[8] The concerted focus on valuing the Black family as a space of sustainably, pride, and community preservation grew out of centuries of institutional racism aimed directly at tearing apart Black families. Separating Black mothers from their children was a foundational element of American slavery. Denying the human right of parenting one's children was part and parcel of denying one's right to identity.[9]

When Austin was thirty-six and had decided to adopt a child, her experience with Black adoption facilitated her ability to have compassion and understanding for birth mothers. She loved her own mother, who had struggled to parent: "If we judged the parents for their shortcomings, we are actively judging the very children we want to serve. Even if we never directly say 'your father is a jailbird,' our negative energy might imply that the little boy is lucky to have been removed from his family and put into more reliable hands."[10]

Austin entered the foster-to-adoption process through the Los Angeles County system in 2006 with a unique level of understanding of the complexities of adoption. She was a successful, professional writer and a single Black woman. She did not fit the standard of who society says is valued and even capable of single parenting—not because of her abilities, education, knowledge, and stability, but because of her race. As Austin navigated the courses and complex bureaucratic foster-to-adopt system, the duplicity of the system meant to best serve children and families became more and more visible to her: "I was particularly annoyed that Black foster mothers were painted in large, ugly brush strokes while the whites-as-saviors-of-Black-children narrative reigned supreme. All the feel-good movies with white foster mothers like *Losing Isaiah* were warm, loving, and devoted to the Black child they were saving, while the Black mothers shown in the media were crackheads or some other form of trash straight out of the Black-woman-stereotype guide."[11] The pernicious binary of adoption in America, in which white moms are saviors and Black moms are incompetent, perpetuates this powerful narrative of who is worthy and unworthy of mothering.

Austin's eventual adoption of her Black son, August, who was six months old when Austin began fostering him, would be the platform from which she would define motherhood—on her terms and in opposition to all the micro and macro stereotypes that society threw in her path. While she entered the steep learning curve of parenting, Austin found that there were no resources, no literature, no handbooks, no how-to guides for her, a Black mother raising an adopted Black son. In fact, there were almost no handbooks for Black mothers in general. "As a writer, I was fighting against white privilege's erasure of Black parenting perspectives and insistence that the mother automatically meant white. The denial of voices of color meant our children's lives did not matter."[12] And so Austin bravely took on the double-burdened task of not only parenting as a single mother but also fighting to redefine how America saw her value and right to mother, as a Black woman, on her terms. Her memoir is a call for this fundamental change.

The historical foundations of adoption in the United States are rooted in restricted, destructive, and blatantly bigoted assumptions about who is a good mother and who is a bad one. These foundations expose our culture's deep distrust of women and help explain the subtle and not-so-subtle challenges Austin and millions of women and mothers have faced. There are deep roots that have, over time, profoundly shaped who is acceptable and unacceptable to mother in America and how adoption and sterilization have been used to enforce these normative assumptions around hegemonic motherhood. Deviation from that acceptable identity and path results in sometimes subversive and sometimes direct shaming of the deviant mother. American women, especially women of color, have been told that they may not keep their babies, or have been forcibly sterilized so they do not have more children. They have been told that they are unworthy of mothering. At the same time, white middle-class women have been repeatedly told that they are unworthy if they choose not to mother, cannot have babies, or become pregnant out of wedlock. All American women live within the tension of this paradox, which only allows a small window of acceptable motherhood, of acceptable womanhood.

In 1974, the year before I was born, the state of North Carolina ended a decades-old program of forcibly sterilizing people, predominantly women and girls of color, under the justification of easing the financial burden on state-run public services, as opposed to moral or ethical reasons. By 1960, 60 percent of those sterilized were Black, and 99 percent were female.[13] At the culmination of this horrific and unjust sterilization program, several thousand citizens had been sterilized under the pretext that it was "good for them and good for society."[14]

During the 1960s and 1970s, there was a drastic decrease in the availability of healthy white babies for adoption. This resulted from several major societal and legal changes that emerged in these decades. The sexual revolution of the 1960s, coupled with increased access to birth control, pushed against the boundaries of what was expected of young, adult women in terms of both sexual behavior and marital expectations. And the landmark 1973 Supreme Court decision *Roe v. Wade* opened the doors to safe and accessible abortions. At this pivotal time, there was a confluence of more unwed women choosing to keep their babies, as society's rigid perceptions of acceptable motherhood began to fissure. In 1970, 80 percent of children born out of wedlock were given up for adoption. By 1983, fewer than 4 percent of unwed mothers made that decision.[15] Young women were also taking control of their reproductive rights by decisively opting to not get pregnant while being sexually active, to use birth control, and to terminate unplanned pregnancies safely and legally.

A look back at specific policies that targeted women into the early twentieth century, especially women of reproductive age, helps explain the circumstances during the period in which I was born and adopted out. These policies and programs all impacted how young women could or could not mother, who was allowed to mother, and the rigid societally prescribed role a valued, acceptable mother must play in American society. In the early twentieth century, "good mothers" were a precondition for healthy citizens and a strong democracy. The social enforcement of the good mother identity during this time unironically coincided with the increased regulation of adoption practices as well as the apex of the eugenics movement. As the societal noose tightened around who could mother and who could not and how mothering should be done, so did the noose around the necks of those deemed unworthy of participating in American society. At the center of all these confines sat the American family.

The North Carolina sterilization program provides a lens through which we can see, with clarity, how our nation differentially values humans, particularly mothers and babies. The program determined who was fit to be a mother. It highlighted the barriers to accessing who was privileged to be celebrated as a mother and what types of babies were wanted and not wanted. North Carolina was not the only state in the nation to run pervasive sterilization programs. Every state in the nation had forced sterilization programs, and thirty states had eugenics-inspired laws, leading to the sterilization of over sixty thousand United States citizens.[16] In fact, California, where I was born, led the nation with more than twenty-one thousand sterilizations. Virginia was second with eight thousand, and North Carolina came third.[17] But what makes the North Carolina program stand out is that it was the longest and most aggressive of all the state-run programs. In fact, the North Carolina laws that allowed for these sterilization programs would not be formally repealed until 2003.[18]

North Carolina's sterilization program, like those of other US states, began in the early 1920s, in the heyday of the eugenics movement. Eugenicists argued that good genes, or "good blood," would determine human traits such as intelligence, sexuality, criminality, and one's general success or failure as a civic member of society. The elimination of bad genes from the population, eugenicists argued, all but ensured that future generations of Americans would flourish.[19] Superficially, this pseudoscience claimed the practice would help eliminate illnesses and medical deficiencies by purifying bloodlines. But in reality, its goal was rooted in deep-seated racism and bigotry, and its proponents and founders upheld an idealized vision of a white, heteronormative, middle-class Protestant family. According to eugenics, the highest-quality genes, or bloodlines, were Nordic. Northern European bloodlines produced the best men and women, who produced the best families.[20] In the world of eugenics, deviance and illegitimacy were rooted in racial identity, not actual behavior or ability.

North Carolina eugenics laws, originally passed in 1929, allowed for sterilization for three reasons: epilepsy, sickness, and "feeblemindedness." It was this category of feeblemindedness that opened the door for political leaders, doctors, and social workers to justify the sterilization of poor Black women simply because they were poor and Black. Between 1929 and 1968, nearly 72 percent of all sterilizations were made in the case of feeblemindedness.[21]

"Feeblemindedness," a now-defunct and pejorative term, was at the time a classification for people who were considered mentally inferior. It was used by eugenicists and many others also as a label for people who were considered sexually deviant, particularly those who engaged in sexual activity outside of wedlock and for personal pleasure. And women, especially poor, uneducated women of color, became the primary targets of this classification. As journalism professor Harry Bruinius writes in his historical account of forced sterilization in America, "Biologically speaking, science was revealing perhaps the greatest menace to the future of the human race: fecund, feebleminded females."[22] The power to procreate, held by the "wrong" women, became twisted into a criminal shame of overfertility and mental deviance. In the 1927 Supreme Court decision *Buck v. Bell*, the court upheld Virginia's eugenics sterilization program. Justice Oliver Wendell Holmes Jr., writing for the Court's majority, opined that the United States would be "swamped with incompetence" if feebleminded women were allowed to reproduce.

This nebulous classification of feebleminded allowed authorities to haphazardly determine who needed to be sterilized. In most cases, these decisions were made by social workers who had little or no medical training and were poorly equipped to judge the complex situations the people before them faced. North Carolina was the only state that allowed social workers to personally recommend people for sterilization. And those they picked, predominantly girls and women of color, would then stand before a panel of five bureaucrats from the state eugenics board who, within a matter of minutes, would decide whether the woman was worthy of being a mother.

In the records from these board hearings, in which the lives and values of young women were decided, the subjectivity of determining feeblemindedness is stunning. The grounds on which young women, and even girls, were being classified as feebleminded and then forcibly sterilized included:

"She wears men's clothing all the time." (1947)
"Her mother says that she did not go to school as regularly as she could because she had sleep spells and slight attacks of epilepsy." (1954)
"She seems lazy and unconcerned." (1960)
"While in school attempted to write love letters to boys she imagined were interested in her." (1962)[23]

The irony of the eugenics movement, which rested in a belief that nature is more powerful than nurture, was that it helped fuel adoption in the United States. Even today, the foundational philosophy of adoption is that nurture can be more influential than nature. A good mother and father can raise an adopted baby to become a moral and productive member of society, regardless of the circumstances of that baby's birth or birth family. Yet eugenics argued the opposite: that people of certain races and deficiencies, such as feeblemindedness, would inevitably pass on their genetic immortality and depravity. The expansion of the eugenics movement and sterilization programs dovetailed with maternalist reformers of the early and mid-twentieth century who wanted to clean up the urban ghettos, sanitize the influx of dark-skinned immigrants who were flooding into the United States, and save the future of the nation by reforming immigrants' babies and children.

During this period, particularly through the Great Depression, as widespread unemployment and rampant poverty spread across the country, many social reformers saw the American family as the cause and solution to society's ills: "Amidst this sense of diminished manhood and alongside a perceived crisis in liberalism, the family came to function as a yardstick for measuring political health more than as a private or self-enclosed unit."[24] Eighty-two percent of respondents in a 1936 Gallup poll agreed that married women who worked outside the home were "thieving parasites" who took men's jobs away.[25] The restrictive lanes of hegemonic mothering narrowed as it became more and more deviant for women to be working mothers. For women, particularly white middle-class women who could not become pregnant after they dutifully walked down the aisle, this presented a real crisis. And as the ideal of the American family became more entrenched, so did adoptions and, paradoxically, sterilization programs that targeted Black, Brown, and Indigenous women.

As sterilization programs proliferated around the country, so did adoption programs. Between 1937 and 1945, adoptions increased from 16,000 to 50,000 annually. And by 1965, there were 142,000 adoptions annually.[26] At the root of both was a distrust of women—of bad women, and their inability to mother, and, paradoxically, of good women mothering appropriately. My birth and adoption in 1975 followed on the heels of decades of sterilization programs nationwide that valued white mothers and babies over mothers and babies of color. These racist policies influenced adoption trends that favored the adoption of white babies.

By the mid-twentieth century, as sterilization programs proliferated nationwide and adoption practices were reaching a zenith, the hegemonic American family came to be seen as the antidote to all social, political, and economic ills. As historian Ruth Feldstein writes, "In these years, motherhood assumed meaning in relation to assumptions that Americans had about families, gender roles, racial difference, and the role of the federal government. Representations of women as mothers developed in conjunction with the debates about who was a healthy citizen and what was a healthy democracy."[27] American mothers were carrying the weight and responsibility of the entire democracy. This meant that women who didn't operate within the acceptable confines of American motherhood were seen as an enormous, existential threat to the nation. And for decades to come, this mentality would give license to lawmakers, social service workers, and legal experts not only to prevent women from becoming mothers but also to take babies from women deemed deviant and irresponsible.

The same year I was born, 1975, David and Louisa Rendon, a White Earth Chippewa couple from Minnesota, stood before a judge in Texas, where David was doing migrant work in the oil fields, begging to keep custody of their infant son. Their baby boy had been born premature but healthy. While he was still in the hospital, the Texas Welfare Department obtained a court order to take him away from David and Louisa on the grounds that they were not prepared to care for him. Social workers with the Texas Welfare Department came to this conclusion because the couple had not yet bought a crib for their baby, who was born prematurely, and because David, as a migrant worker, was gone too much from home. Thus, they argued, these parents should permanently lose custody of their infant. Louisa, the social workers noted, "would probably neglect this child."[28] Although the judge finally ruled in favor of the Rendons, he told their attorney during a court break that he would give the couple their infant son back in thirty days but stated, "I don't care what they do with this child; they can barbecue the child for all I care."[29] Between the 1950s and 1970s, thousands of horrifying cases like the Rendons' played out for Indigenous families across the United States.

The brutality that Indigenous women faced in courtrooms, hospital rooms, and the back rooms of state social services offices, where they were manipulated and coerced into relinquishing their babies, echoes the same levels of disdainful shame other women of color faced in motherhood. Social scientists and historians reference that in the early to mid-1900s, the United States grappled with the "Indian problem" and the "Negro problem."[30] Fundamental in this bigoted paradigm was the "mother of color" problem. Social systems and policies targeted young women of color, seeing their potential fertility as a threat to society and the boundaries of acceptable motherhood.

Indigenous women, like Black women, were and continue to be stigmatized as paradoxically too fertile yet incapable of mothering. From the post–World War II era to the 1970s, when adoption was booming in America, women of color were held up to ideals of correct, acceptable mothering and family structures set by a middle-class, white standard. And women who failed to fit into this ideal, particularly because of out-of-wedlock pregnancies, were considered mentally unstable and deviant and could not be trusted to raise their children. As Margaret Jacobs explains in her complex and moving account of Indigenous adoption in the mid-twentieth century, "Unwed Indian mothers, however, experienced a qualitatively different public attitude than white women who had children out of wedlock. Indian motherhood became virtually synonymous with unwed pregnancy in the eyes of non-Indians. Many outside observers did not regard Indian custom marriages as legitimate. . . . These views led to commonplace assumptions that by definition an Indian mother was unwed and therefore psychologically unstable and unfit."[31]

The tragic irony of these caustic assumptions about Indigenous mothering is that it lacks any understanding of how many Indigenous communities have and continue to authentically approach childrearing. For many Indigenous communities, the act of childrearing is a community project that involves multigenerational support. The significant mentors in an Indigenous child's life could be an auntie or elder who may not even be an immediate family member. The activity of community childrearing is so intrinsic to many Indigenous communities that it is understood as a form of resistance to state intervention.[32] The preservation and sustainability of the tribal community offer resistance to colonizing forces that have sought to destroy Indigenous culture for centuries. Thus, protecting, mentoring, and guiding Indigenous youth is an important act involving the entire community.

Indigenous perceptions of family and parenting dramatically contradict the hegemonic American perceptions of family and what it means to care for Indigenous children. Most significantly, the concept of being illegitimate has never been part of many Indigenous tribal communities. In her study of gender and power in tribal communities on the Columbia Plateau in the Pacific Northwest, Lillian Ackerman explains, "A child born to a young single woman was accepted by the mother's kin without condemnation. Such a situation was neither a social nor a psychological handicap in a child's life; nor was the mother criticized. She either kept the child or allowed it to be adopted by a married couple. If she kept the child it was easily integrated into the non-unilinear descent group."[33] Many Indigenous communities have held onto these values of tribal support and wraparound care for youth, carrying the traditions of old ways into contemporary times. Sarah Newcomb, a member of the Tsimshian Tribe of Alaska, echoes this same perspective of childrearing without the concepts of shame and illegitimacy. She writes,

> In Tsimshian culture there was no such thing as an illegitimate child. The word simply didn't exist, because there was no need for it, as this belief didn't exist. All children were legitimate. All children simply belonged to the people, specifically, they belonged to the clan of the birth mother and followed her matriarchal lineage. There was also no such thing as a single mother, not in the way we think of it. Single mothers, illegitimate children, etc., none of this was cultural. It all came with colonization. Regardless of the invention of such words, all children were and are legitimate.[34]

When a community has no need for the word "illegitimate," there is no shame in mothering and parenting. What mothering and parenting look like is fluid and flexible, rooted in the needs of each individual child and mother.

But forces outside tribal communities continue to pressure Indigenous and other nonwhite communities to adhere to a hegemonic form of mothering that justifies the condemnation and even sterilization of those deemed "bad" or unacceptable mothers. The forced or coerced sterilization of Indigenous women, Black and Brown women, poor women, and women living with HIV continues to this day in the United States. Women are forced to consent to sterilization procedures under situations of duress, under false or misinformed pretenses, and even with no consent at all.[35] A licensed practical nurse at an Immigration and Customs Enforcement (ICE) detention center in Georgia in 2020 filed a whistleblower complaint of forced hysterectomies on detained women. Advocates from the South Georgia Immigrant Support Network testified, "With alarming frequency we hear about women who've received gynecological procedures. Sometimes they were not given an opportunity to give consent for that." Some of the women in the center were not properly informed about the procedure's outcomes and did not fully comprehend that they had been sterilized.[36] This case is emblematic of a larger trend of distrusting and demonizing Black and Brown immigrant women and the extent to which government entities will go to inhibit women's rights to fertility autonomy out of fear and distrust. That this case in Georgia happened in an ICE facility also speaks to a bigoted trope of immigrant mothers bringing their swollen pregnant bellies across the border to give birth in American hospitals. Fertility continues to be a threat to the American way of life.

My birth mother's experience as a young, white, unmarried woman dealing with an accidental pregnancy in 1975 was also impacted by historical assumptions about good versus bad motherhood and good versus bad womanhood. An unplanned pregnancy for an unmarried woman was not considered good for most families, regardless of race, class, or faith. For decades, the way white communities dealt with the problem of unplanned pregnancies was to shuttle pregnant girls and young women away in secrecy to sit out their pregnant days in maternity homes with other young women, each waiting her turn to give birth, then to hand away her baby to an anxiously awaiting couple, desperate for a chance to have a family. These girls were then expected to return to high school or college as if nothing had happened. This history, much like my birth, is defined by secrecy and familial shame.

Post–World War II America experienced a massive economic boom that would, in part, help solidify what the ideal American family was supposed to look like. The rigidity of this image necessitated secrecy and shame in any family that failed to uphold the boundaries of this image. By the mid-1950s, nearly 60 percent of the population enjoyed a middle-class income, compared to 30 percent before the Great Depression. The federal government encouraged returning veterans to purchase single-family homes in booming suburbs by offering generous home loans. In 1947 alone, 800,000 veterans received home loans through the GI Bill. But the dark lining of this economic and social prosperity was the increasing, stifling pressure for families to conform to middle-class standards. The perfect nuclear family was the gold standard to which everyone who wanted success needed to adhere. During the 1950s and 1960s, the percentage of the population that was married skyrocketed. By 1960, 68 percent of the US population was married. Families were living the suburban American dream.[37]

With this idealized family came the proliferation of shame and stigma around unplanned pregnancy, as it directly threatened the ideal of the nuclear, hegemonic family. As a result, maternity home systems, secret places where young, white unwed girls could silently wait out their pregnancies, have their babies in secrecy, relinquish them for adoption, and then return to their middle-class homes and schools, also proliferated around the country.[38]

Maternity homes were the successors of homes run by organizations doing "rescue work" for girls and women in the late 1800s. Two of the largest organizations, the Salvation Army and the Florence Crittenton Mission, advertised their work as offering shelter and redemption for "fallen women," including prostitutes and homeless and unwed mothers. In the 1950s, as the middle class swelled—and with it, the idealized nuclear family—these organizations' focus narrowed to middle-class white girls, considered the most redeemable.

A philosophical paradigm drove this system. Motherhood was synonymous with marriage. Pregnancy outside marriage was shameful. For a young, unmarried pregnant girl to get back into "good girl" status, she had to relinquish her baby in secret. The Florence Crittenton Mission, the Salvation Army, and other organizations ran more than two hundred maternity homes in forty-four states. In the mid-1950s, about 40 percent of first births to girls aged fifteen to nineteen were conceived out of wedlock. By 1974, that number had reached 60 percent. At this point, these maternity homes were operating at maximum capacity and regularly turning applicants away.[39] Collectively, these homes could house twenty-five thousand girls a year, and as many as 35 percent of their applicants were turned away.

The cost of housing at a Salvation Army maternity home by the mid-1960s was $100 a month, with additional fees charged for delivery. A stay through the duration of a pregnancy and birth could cost a family nearly $1,500. Even for middle-class families, this was a significant financial burden. The wealth and opportunity that arose for many American families in the post–World War II era, which made the excessive costs of these programs accessible, were largely inaccessible to families of color. The middle-class dream was largely out of reach for many Black communities, even Black GIs who had given so much during the war. Redlining policies, supported by the Federal Housing Authority, prevented Black families from accessing government loans and purchasing single-family homes in booming suburbs around the country in the 1950s and 1960s. This institutional racism was also visible in maternity homes. They became places that served primarily white girls, who, in the minds of organizational leaders, could be most easily rehabilitated. In 1952, the Florence Crittenton organization reported that only a third of the maternity homes across the country provided services for Black girls, and three were "solely for Negro girls."[40]

Societal perceptions of a good girl and how disruptive pregnancy impacted this identity were experienced differently by white girls and girls of color. Who was allowed the privilege of being a good girl and the narrow path of staying in this role once pregnant were largely determined by one's race and class. Although the daily routines and experiences at different maternity homes varied widely, one commonality among women interviewed years after their time spent in these homes was a pervasive feeling of fear and abandonment. Most of these girls had never spent time away from home in their young lives. Here, they were forced away into isolation during one of the most profound experiences of their lives: pregnancy and birth. Despite the powerful networks of friendship that the girls in the homes developed as they went through their pregnancies, the experiences were traumatic. These girls had been shunned by their families, churches, and communities because of the grievous misstep of an unplanned pregnancy, which threatened their family's connection to the perfect nuclear-family paradigm.[41]

In *Embroidering the Scarlet A: Unwed Mothers and Illegitimate Children in American Fiction and Film*, literary scholar Janet Mason Ellerby traces the evolution of the "fallen woman" through literary fiction and film. Ellerby shares her own moving testimonial of being forced away to a maternity home to carry out her pregnancy and give up her baby while she was a high school student in 1965. The same year she was pregnant, she read *The Scarlet Letter* in English class and felt a deep connection to the book's main character, Hester Prynne. As Ellerby explains,

> Although women today have greater cultural and political power, unmarried women who have sex are still not free from social opprobrium, and their right to choose an abortion is by no means forever guaranteed, and even so, the increasing number of women who choose motherhood outside of marriage face many fewer social penalties. Nevertheless, dependent, unwed teen mothers are still pressured to surrender their babies to adoption, and although most American adoptions are now either open (i.e., the adoptee grows up knowing at least one of her birthparents) or mediated,

that shift has not led to an opening of all adoption records. In the majority of states, they remain firmly closed. The disgrace of having an out-of-wedlock pregnancy has diminished, but the moral values the "Scarlet A" symbolized are still with us, and with me. I have never been able to fully conquer the shame that unwed motherhood ignited in me. In 1965 I saw Hester as an enviable model; I still do. But decades of painful experience have taught me a sobering lesson: Hester is more a misleading fantasy than a realistic role model.[42]

I do not know if my birth mother spent time in a maternity home or some other isolated location throughout her pregnancy with me, or if she continued to walk the halls of her law school while her belly swelled conspicuously. I do, however, know that her family saw my coming as a burden that needed to be dealt with, which is why she was pressured to pursue my adoption in secrecy. My adoptive parents have told me that my birth father was also a law student, a classmate of my mother's. What is obvious is that he did not have to endure the shame and stigma of a distended body while he toiled in class, preparing for exams. The thought of an unplanned child did not create professional roadblocks for his life and plans to the extent they did for my birth mother. I don't even know if he knew of my conception and birth. His part in my conception was fleeting and minimal in terms of responsibility. He was not condemned by his actions to the colossal level my birth mother was.

One woman who, at the age of sixteen, gave birth and relinquished her baby at a maternity home reflected upon her painful and confusing experience:

I remember thinking I wished it [my baby] was a boy, because boys can't have children. I thought, "I gave birth to a little girl who's going to have to go through this, that poor little thing." I had always thought boys had it better than women. All my life, you know? And that whole experience made me feel even more so—that it's the girls who get punished, the girls who suffer through all of this stuff, and the girls who can't talk about it.[43]

When I learned I was pregnant with my first baby, I had a deep secret wish that this baby would be a boy. My husband was the only son of his parents, and I desperately wanted to present my in-laws with an heir to the family name, the prodigal son that our society celebrates. I believed with all my heart that this tiny baby growing inside me was a boy, that magical son. I remember being absolutely stunned to learn in the eighteen-week ultrasound that she was a girl. What I struggled with most while I lay on the hospital table, the cold, wet ultrasound transducer pushing back and forth across my belly, was this deep sense of shame that I had wanted her to be a boy.

I never told anyone that I had wished for a boy. I felt so ashamed for falling prey to the societal expectation that I could birth a prodigal son who could seamlessly evade any guilt, shame, or trauma associated with fertility and motherhood. Cognitively, I didn't believe any of that crap. But emotionally, I felt the pressure of it. I also felt this deep fear that this tiny girl growing inside of me would someday be judged for either growing a baby or not growing a baby inside her own belly. I was afraid for my baby girl just as the woman who relinquished her newborn girl at the maternity home felt fear for her baby girl. Mostly, I didn't want my baby to ever face the decision to give up her own baby, as my birth mother had done.

5

Death

On the night of August 19, 2017, my husband woke me up to tell me my mom was on the phone. It was late, and I had just fallen asleep. When he handed me the phone, I was still in that half-asleep realm, disconnected from reality. My husband looked strange. His face was totally blank, which is not a normal expression for him. I can generally identify his emotional state based on his face. This night I saw nothing, and a wave of nausea swept into the depths of my gut. I took the phone and said hi to my mom. She said my sister, Rachel, was dead.

The morning before my sister died, she was scheduled to have shoulder surgery. She had been looking forward to this procedure for months. We had last seen her in February of that year, and even then, she was talking about how excited she was about the surgery. Rachel had come to a place in her life where she sought refuge in hospitals. When she was in the hospital, she felt loved. Nurses, doctors, and various specialists consistently cared for her, asking what she needed, where it hurt, and what could ease the pain. Hospitals and surgery meant pain relief in the form of nurses who cared for her unconditionally, without judgment of her past mistakes. It also meant relief in the form of narcotics. The older my sister grew, the greater her pain became. And by the time she hit her early forties, narcotics were all that brought her relief and escape.

An hour before the surgery was scheduled to begin, the anesthesiologist called it off. He was concerned about Rachel's ability to come out of the anesthesia. She had a lot of substances lingering in her already-fragile system, and the anesthesiologist didn't want a corpse on the operating table. That afternoon, Rachel left the hospital in a fury. She needed this surgery like a baby needed her mother. She wanted to feel warm and cared for, and to have the sweet relief of painkillers calming her down. That night, alone in her apartment, Rachel sought relief in what she had available: alcohol and sleeping pills. She died of a drug overdose late that same night. The corpse wasn't on the operating table—it was on the bed. The next morning, her neighbor found her swollen, soiled body laying contorted on the bed. My sister died alone and in physical pain. But it was the mental and emotional pain that had been building up for decades, piled up heavily on top of her worn-out, crippled body, that finally crushed her.

Rachel was never able to mother on her own terms or see her fertility as a blessing, a strength, or something she had autonomy over. As a sexually active teenager, she was told that her fertility was a problem that had to be controlled. As she grew older, she saw it as a burden and a painful memory of the mistakes she had made as a mother. When my sister was a teenager, our parents forced her to have a Norplant contraceptive device embedded into her arm. She attempted to carve it out using a razor blade. I do not know how many times my sister became pregnant. I know she had at least one abortion. She gave birth to two babies, a boy in 1999 and a girl in 2005, both with different fathers. Rachel lost custody of her son when he was five. At the time, she was using drugs and drinking. The final straw for her son's dad and the county was when she picked her son up from school drunk. She was going off the rails with her drug use, and she was failing epically at safely raising her son.

After Rachel lost custody of her son, her drug abuse and path of self-destruction only intensified. After an orchestrated family intervention with our parents, myself, and the father of her son, Rachel headed off to what would be her final stint in rehab. When she returned home several months later, sober and clearer than she had been in years, Rachel reconnected with an old friend and became pregnant with her daughter. Her daughter was the love child between Rachel and a dynamic, handsome man whom she had been friends with and loved for years. She gave her newborn up for adoption right after birth, just like Rachel's birth mother had done with her. Relinquishing this love child, this precious baby girl, crushed Rachel. I don't know if social workers coaxed Rachel into giving her daughter up for adoption. At that time, she and I were not talking—I didn't even know she was pregnant. I understand now that regardless of what anyone was telling her, as she made the decision to give up her baby, she was immersed in tremendous shame and guilt. As a result, she cut everybody out of her life. The state had taken away her son, whom she loved fiercely but struggled to parent. She was a known addict. The relinquishment of her second baby was inevitable.

Adoption is made possible because a pregnant woman isn't able to mother, consciously chooses to forgo mothering, or—even now, in a stunning number of cases—is told she cannot mother and her child is taken from her. Rachel's life as a mother who lost custody of both of her children was a complex mix of all these scenarios. An entire profession whose aim is to support children and families has a problematic history of not just taking babies and children from mothers but also doing so in abusive and subversive ways. The duplicity of the history of social work itself demonstrates the pervasive nature of our nation's assumptions about who is worthy of mothering and who is not, and how social systems should intervene to help and support those in need. Social workers have enormous power as mediators and conduits in the transfer of babies and children from one family to another. As one New York State child welfare official bluntly stated in

1960, "Every time we place a child for adoption, we feel like we're playing God, with all the hazards of playing God."[1]

The objectives of the social work profession have changed over the past century as adoption policies have vacillated between family preservation and family separation. But one consistent pattern in the policies and on-the-ground practices of social workers in family services is that family preservation efforts have been afforded to some and intentionally withheld from others. Also consistent is the enormous power one or a few individuals within the social work profession have to assess and evaluate mothers, literally determining who can and cannot mother, sometimes based on an incredibly small amount of subjective data. Lastly, the role of social workers in adoption scenarios has also revolved around assimilationist agendas. Social workers have labored to assimilate families deemed worthy of preservation into acceptable American ideals. And they have also separated families, taking babies and children away when birth mothers and birth communities were deemed unassimilable.

The first university-level social work course offered was at Columbia University in 1898. By the early 1900s, universities around the nation offered a wide cadre of social work courses. This new profession, inspired by the pioneering work of Jane Addams, promised to address the public needs of America's most vulnerable people by providing aid to immigrants, to those in poverty, and to those experiencing abuse and neglect. It is not a coincidence that the birth of social work as an institutionalized profession happened in tandem with the US government's regulation of child care, adoptions, and orphanages in the early 1900s and the creation of the USCB in 1912, followed by the CWLA in 1921. These social service institutions would be run by newly minted, aspirational social workers, the vast majority of whom were white, middle-class Protestant men and women. This original cohort of social work professionals comprised "members of a set of loosely connected movements, Progressives [who] set about to regulate big business, democratize and reform the political system, aid the urban poor and exploited workers, and impose homogeneous cultural values on the entire population, especially Catholic and Jewish immigrants and blacks."[2] Women and children were originally—and continue to be—the most prevalent recipients of social welfare services.

Early-twentieth-century welfare policies focused on family preservation. This was a direct response to pervasive conditions of destitute urban poverty, experienced most poignantly by single mothers. These conditions led to the baby and child trafficking that permeated the turn of the previous century, when orphan trains, baby farms, and outright child abductions were common. In 1900, 9 percent of all children lived with one parent; in most cases, that parent was their mother.[3] Between 1900 and 1910, single mothers typically earned two to four dollars a week, working incredibly low-wage domestic service jobs. Their dual responsibilities as childcare givers and wage earners left these single mothers in situations of destitute poverty and left their children vulnerable to kidnapping and abuse. A social worker in 1909 described the living conditions of a poor, single, working mother in New York City's Lower East Side:

> You live in three rooms in Essex street. . . . There is a boarder who helps out with the rent. . . . You only have one bed. The boarder must have it. The three older children slept on a mattress on the floor after she brought them in from the street at eleven o'clock. The baby who is only eight months old, slept with you on the fire escape, and you stayed awake half the night for fear you might lose your hold on him and he might fall. Willie has a running nose and they tell you at the day nursery that if its [sic] not better today you will have to keep him home. . . . That means that Nellie will have to stay away form [sic] school and take care of him. You are only thirty-six years old, but you look forty-nine.[4]

Single mothers stuck in unbreakable cycles of poverty, unable to safely house and care for their children, were easy victims of a system of family separation at a time when there were virtually no services to support them. In 1909, the White House Conference on the Care of Dependent Children reported that 93,000 children lived in orphanages and children's homes, 50,000 lived in foster homes, and 25,000 in juvenile detention centers.[5]

In 1911, Progressive social welfare reformers created "mothers' pensions." The policy was to give poor women pensions so that they could provide for their children at home. Progressive welfare reformers championed mothers and the importance of nurturing children in safe, healthy environments. Mothers' pensions became the first formal, government-subsidized program to promote family preservation. By 1935, every state except South Carolina and Georgia had passed mothers' pension laws. Through the Social Security Act, the federal government assumed responsibility for partially funding these state-based programs under the umbrella of the Aid to Families with Dependent Children (AFDC) program. The AFDC would run until it was terminated in 1996, becoming one of the oldest social welfare programs in the nation's history.[6]

But this early welfare policy, aimed at keeping families together through state-subsidized support, was decidedly exclusive regarding who was determined eligible to be saved and supported. This exclusionary approach was echoed in the very 1909 White House Conference on the Care of Dependent Children that also highlighted the severity of the situation in terms of the number of children taken out of poor homes. The conference concluded:

> Children of parents of worthy character, suffering from temporary misfortune, and children of reasonably efficient and deserving mothers who are without the support of the normal breadwinner, should as a rule, be kept with their par-

ents, such aid being given as may be necessary to maintain suitable homes for the rearing of children. . . . Except in unusual circumstances, the home should not be broken up for reasons of poverty, but only for considerations of inefficiency or immorality.[7]

With the rollout of mothers' pensions, the single mothers who qualified as worthy of character and those deemed immoral and inefficient were largely based on the bigoted assumptions of the very social workers and policymakers who professed to help sustain and hold families together. Caseworkers, who had the power to determine a family's fitness for criteria to access these funds, regularly excluded Black and non–Northern European mothers.[8] By 1931, only 3 percent of all families given access to mothers' pensions were Black. The criteria for acceptance were even lower for unwed mothers—a 1933 study found that fewer than 0.1 percent of mothers' pensions were awarded to unwed, "illegitimate" mothers.[9] The vast majority of payment recipients, those deemed worthy of saving, were white, widowed mothers.

The babies and children of the families disqualified from AFDC care were placed into the growing foster care system. They fed the mounting demand for adoptable babies in both public and private adoption agencies. Historian Deborah Ward highlights the subjective criteria by which social workers within state systems were determining whether a woman was fit to mother, what was a suitable home, who was fit to run it, and the link between these criteria and assumptions about the ability of the recipients to assimilate into American cultural norms: "[T]he programs functioned in a way that systematically excluded African-Americans and were only provisionally available to those immigrants willing or able to Americanize."[10] Social workers in social welfare programs, including the AFDC's mothers' pensions and eugenics-inspired sterilization programs of the 1920s, 1930s, and 1940s, were crafting the

image of what was an acceptable and valued family in America
and, on a grassroots level, determining who and who could not
participate in that American family archetype.

The end of World War II would mark a transition period in
social work practices, particularly in the area of adoption. This
was the beginning of what many historians call the Baby Scoop
Era, a period between 1945 and the early 1970s characterized by
an increase in premarital pregnancies and the nation's highest
rates of domestic adoptions. The social work profession played a
pivotal role in the evolution of the Baby Scoop Era in several fundamental ways. Most notably, this period would mark a fundamental shift in social welfare policy away from family preservation
and toward family separation and the forced relinquishment of
babies.

A convergence of trends fed into this change in social work during the Baby Scoop Era. First, by 1945, there was an enormous
spike in women entering the field of social work.[11] Huge numbers
of young women were studying social work in college as it was
emerging as one of the few reputable, financially sustainable, and
accessible professional fields available to educated women. Second, adoption rates rose dramatically in the post–World War II
years, and private adoption agencies and maternity homes were
becoming lucrative businesses. Social work, especially social work
practiced by young, educated white women, was becoming heavily
integrated into the business of adoption.[12]

An army of young, college-educated women, who were predominantly white, filled the staffing rolls at maternity homes,
private adoption agencies, and public social service organizations.
These young social workers were making profound, life-altering
decisions for thousands of young pregnant women. As these
changes were taking place societally, the objectives of social work
were fundamentally altering. In the pre–World War II years,
family preservation was the objective for those families deemed
worthy. Now, under the authority of science and research, family

separation became the front-facing objective in social work practices. In previous decades, single mothers had been disqualified from social services because of their illegitimate status as unmarried mothers. Now they were directly targeted by social services for forced relinquishment of their babies. And there was a growing industry with orchestrated systems of funneling babies from birth mothers to the arms of adoptive parents.

What helped facilitate this transition toward family separation, particularly the belief that separating the newborn baby from its birth mother and coercing relinquishment was the best scenario for an illegitimate pregnancy, was an "evolution in the perception of unmarried mothers among social workers, changing from 'seduced and abandoned' to 'feebleminded' and then to 'sex delinquents.' Social work professionals began to see unmarried mothers as dangerous rather than as endangered."[13] The unmarried, young pregnant woman became the enemy, and her baby had to be saved from her. What helped feed this mentality was also the exponentially increasing demand for adoptable babies and the lucrative adoption market that profited off this demand. Between 1942 and 1970, domestic adoption rates skyrocketed from 45,000 to 178,000 adoptions per year.[14]

By the end of the 1950s, the dehumanization of unwed, young birth mothers was institutionalized in social welfare systems. It was standard practice in adoption agencies and maternity homes for social workers to refer to birth mothers as sick and needing punishment for their depravity and immorality. Sara Edlin, the longtime director of the Lakeview Home, a private maternity home on Staten Island, acknowledged this troubling mentality when she wrote that she was "deeply discouraged at the punitive attitude of many social workers and their resistance to any legislation that would make life easier for mother and child."[15] These punitive attitudes manifested into verbal, psychological, and even physical abuse against birth mothers, all aimed at getting these mothers to relinquish their babies for adoption. By the end of the

1960s, in some states an illegitimate pregnancy was considered a crime, and birth mothers could be incarcerated for being pregnant.[16] The threat of incarceration could and was used against birth mothers to coerce them to sign papers giving their babies up for adoption.

The deception and abuse that proliferated in social work practices around adoption during the Baby Scoop Era are stunningly displayed in the story of Margaret Erle Katz, who was forced to relinquish her five-month-old son in 1962. Margaret's story, told in detail in Gabrielle Glaser's book *American Baby*, is particularly shocking, not just in the level of deceit and abusive coercion that trained, professional social workers employed to get Margaret's eventual signature of consent for relinquishment of her son, but even more so because of Margaret's tenacity and courage in resisting relinquishment of her son again and again.

Margaret Erle and George Katz, who were just seventeen and eighteen when their son was born, were committed to each other and their baby son, whom they named Stephen. Even before Stephen was born, with George's stoic support and encouragement, Margaret fought against her mother and a steady stream of social workers who relentlessly harassed, verbally abused, and eventually threatened Margaret into releasing custody of her baby when he was born. Perhaps because Margaret put up such a valiant battle to keep her son, social workers employed those horrific tactics to take him from her.

Margaret's battle began while she was still pregnant and her parents sent her off to the Lakeview Home, one of hundreds around the country that discretely housed young, unwed girls and women while they waited out their pregnancies in secret. Social workers regularly visited the home, befriending the young mothers and quietly counseling them to give their babies up. The social worker to first connect with Margaret, a tall, well-dressed woman in her mid-thirties, had a reputation as a mother figure and confidante. Discretion, trust, and emotional connection were integral to her job, which was to find out the reason for the pregnancy in order to develop an effective strategy for convincing the birth mother to give up the baby.[17] When Margaret resisted the idea of relinquishing her unborn son, the social worker's friendly veneer of compassion and empathy dropped. She asked Margaret, "What have you got to offer this child? You are a teenager."[18] The social worker even told Margaret that she could have her own children someday, children conceived within the sanctity of marriage, in an order and fashion by which Margaret would be validated as a mother. But this baby was conceived in shame, and, in the mind of the social worker, the only way to right that wrong was to transfer that baby to another family, a good family, a valid family.

Amazingly, under these unbelievable attacks, with the support of George, Margaret refused at every turn to sign the relinquishment papers during her stay at Lakeview. Margaret went into labor on December 16, 1961, believing that she had made it through the gauntlet of abusive coercion and would be able to keep her baby boy after he was born. While she was alone at the hospital, unaccompanied by anyone from the maternity home, her family, or even George, and in the throes of painful labor, Margaret was once again pursued by a social worker to sign release forms for her baby. Once again, Margaret refused to sign, even amid contractions, while fear and pain enveloped her.

Margaret's son was immediately whisked away after he was born. When she asked to hold him, an attending nurse replied, "Of course not!" When Margaret persisted, begging to hold this tiny baby she had just birthed, another nurse said, "Look, you're one of the girls from Lakeview. You don't get to hold your baby."[19] The immediate separation of baby from mother was one of the strategies used to force relinquishment. The theory was that if a birth mother didn't have the opportunity to create a bond with her baby, then it would be easier for her to let that baby go. She would be more willing to sign papers.

No birth mother walks away from her baby without trauma. Nearly two decades later, in the late 1970s, Lee Campbell, founder of Concerned United Birthparents (CUB), through her extensive research on birth mothers, would start to change this narrative, showing that this immediate separation between birth mother and baby was equally traumatizing for both mother and baby and would have long-lasting detrimental effects. In that hospital room in 1961, while Margaret watched her newborn be inspected, diapered, and immediately taken away from her, her determination to keep her baby only solidified.

Because Margaret was a minor when her son was born, her mother had the legal authority to sign papers allowing baby Stephen to immediately go into foster care after he was born, which Margaret's mother secretly did. Procedurally, Margaret was supposed to give her consent, as the baby's mother, for this foster transition to happen. But Lakeview, like many maternity homes during the Baby Scoop Era, frequently skirted the rules to ensure an easier transfer of babies. So when Margaret finally returned home from the traumatic birth, her son was officially in the foster care system. Although he could not be legally adopted by another family without Margaret's signed consent, she had no rights to access him either. Margaret would have to beg the social workers who cared for baby Stephen to allow her and his father to visit.

Between Stephen's birth and his eventual adoption, Margaret and George were granted only two, brief visits with their son. In both cases, the attending social workers granted them visitation rights only to get Margaret's signature of relinquishment.[20] On their first visit with their baby, within minutes of holding their son for the first time, George was ushered out of the room, Stephen was taken out of Margaret's arms, and the social worker, who had brought Stephen to his parents, pressed relinquishment papers in Margaret's face, demanding that she sign them. When

Margaret refused once again, the social worker condescendingly and viciously asked her, "When are you going to understand that it will be better for everyone if you just accept this never happened?"[21] Margaret's response was, "He's my baby." She and George left that first visit devasted and in tears, but not without hope. Margaret still had not signed the relinquishment papers.

On their second and final visit with their baby son, Margaret and George were again separated after a few minutes of holding and kissing their baby. This time, George was left with baby Stephen, and Margaret was escorted into a separate room. The social worker tasked with getting her signature pulled out all the stops. Margaret was told that a diplomat wanted to adopt her son that very week. And then the social worker said, "If you don't sign these right now, your child will stay in foster care for God knows how long." Margaret was given the choice of giving her son a privileged life with a wealthy, prestigious family or purgatory in perpetual foster care.

Even at this extreme, Margaret stuck to her conviction that she and George, who were planning to marry, could win their son back, and she said no to signing. With this, the social worker laid out her final threat. "If you don't sign these papers we'll make you a ward of the state. We can put you in juvenile hall. Think of how this will look for your parents. First the pregnancy. Want to get locked up now too?"[22] The story about the diplomat was a flat-out lie. But the social worker did, in fact, have the power to threaten jail time. Under wayward minor codes for juveniles who engaged in "deviant" acts, which included "moral depravity," Margaret could go to jail for having premarital sex as a minor. So under threat of incarceration, Margaret finally crumbled and signed the papers. With her signature, Margaret signed away the final thread of connection delicately bonding her to her son.

Margaret lost all rights to her baby boy two years *after* the National Association of Social Workers approved their very first official code of ethics, which included the passage, "Social work practice is a public trust that requires of its practitioners integrity, compassion, belief in the dignity and worth of human beings, respect for individual differences, a commitment to service, and a dedication to truth."[23] The duplicity is stunning.

As horrific as it is, Margaret's story of losing her son during the Baby Scoop Era is not an outlier. There are thousands of documented cases of young women being coerced by social workers into relinquishing their babies during this period. Even the lies that prompted Margaret to sign away her son were tragically not unique to social work practice at the time.[24] What makes Margaret's story remarkable is the extent to which she resisted the abusive system. Her story is also compelling because of the surprise ending. In a bittersweet, miraculous turn of events over fifty years after Stephen's relinquishment, he and his mother Margaret would reunite. Gabrielle Glaser's meticulous documentation of their story of separation and reunification allows us to see the details of this powerful narrative in technicolor. My sister, Rachel, was born in 1973, at the very end of the Baby Scoop Era; I was born in 1975, when the demand for adoptable babies, especially white babies, had reached its zenith. We were born and adopted in an era of unconscionable practices by social workers, nurses, doctors, attorneys, and other agents who facilitated a booming adoption industry. Lies and deceit defined the industry. The stories we heard our whole lives about our birth mothers and the circumstances of our births may or may not be true. What I am absolutely certain of is that both our birth mothers were in some way shamed for their illegitimate pregnancies and coaxed on some level by social workers or others to give us up.

I grew up being told that Rachel's birth mother used drugs while she was pregnant with her. Whether our parents had empirical evidence of this or rationalized that this must have been the case to explain Rachel's addictions later in her life, I do not know. I was told my whole life that my birth mother was in law school while she was pregnant with me. It is entirely plausible that this was a lie told to my adoptive parents to entice the adoption transaction with the promise of a genetically intelligent baby. This law school story is the one loose thread I have carried my whole life, connecting me to some perceived identity of my birth mother. And it's a thread I must let go of because it is too fragile and uncertain. The one certainty of my and my sister's adoptions is that they were saturated in secrecy. And based on the overwhelmingly prevailing patterns of adoptions during the Baby Scoop Era, our adoptions were also saturated in lies.

In the 1980s and 1990s, the decades following the Baby Scoop Era, domestic adoptions drastically decreased, in part due to women's federally protected reproductive rights with the passage of the *Roe* decision, and in part to shifting societal values that were slower to disgrace single mothers, particularly white single mothers. State after state passed legislation enforcing more open adoption policies. Domestic adoptions were not conducted at the same level of secrecy and shame as they had been in previous decades. But social workers still carried enormous power to make decisions about who was qualified to mother and which families were deemed worthy of social services. This was especially true in the cases of poor women of color.

The mid-1990s marked another transition in social welfare policy that would have especially devastating impacts on Black and Brown mothers and their children. In 1996, President Bill Clinton passed the Personal Responsibility Act, marking the end of the AFDC social program and the beginning of Temporary Assistance for Needy Families (TANF). TANF was a policy response to the growing bigotry and animosity aimed at Black mothers who, particularly under the Reagan administration in the 1980s, were labeled as "welfare queens" and "crack mothers."[25]

Controlling motherhood and fertility has been a century-long component of social welfare in America. Social welfare policy proposals in state houses in the early 1990s, before the passage of TANF, included payments for teen mothers who agreed to have contraceptive implant devices placed in their arms and even requirements for welfare recipients to receive these implants. These extreme policy suggestions, none of which passed, were decidedly directed toward women of color. Health care professionals in the early 1990s regularly coerced Black teenage mothers receiving services through the AFDC to have contraceptive implants embedded in their bodies.

A 1990 editorial in the *Philadelphia Inquirer* directly suggested that social welfare–enforced birth control would lower Black birth rates and decrease poverty.[26] In the 1994 mid-term elections, minority house leader Newt Gingrich, campaigning for the Republican platform Contract with America, decried the horrors of urban America and targeted illegitimate mothers as the root of all problems: "[W]atch any major city local television news. . . . The child abuse, the rape, the murders, the cocaine dealing, the problems of American life are unbelievable. . . . [I]t is impossible to maintain American civilization with 12-year-olds having babies."[27]

The social welfare reform that evolved into the passage of TANF in 1996 aimed to cut down on the "culture of poverty," especially within Black communities, by embedding stringent, often unrealistic work requirements within social support services and ending families' entitlements to cash assistance. In debating the passage of the TANF program, advocates argued that particularly Black mothers needed a "stick" to compel them to take responsibility for raising their children, independent of social welfare.[28]

TANF policies successfully limited families' access to program support, and this disproportionately affected Black and Brown women "who were far more likely than white women to lose benefits because they were sanctioned for not meeting a program rule or reached a time limit."[29] The work requirements embedded in TANF forced many Black and Brown single mothers into low-paying jobs in food service and childcare, dead-ending them in an unsustainable cycle that failed to lift them out of poverty and provide social service support. Stringent sanctions in the TANF system would also cut off entire families, sometimes permanently, from service support if one parent failed to meet work requirements. To date, more than two million families have been cut off from TANF due to work-related sanctions.[30]

The rollout of TANF would have a direct and devastating impact on children, which was not lost on some of the program's biggest advocates. Newt Gingrich described TANF legislation as a measure to "take the children of welfare mothers and put them in orphanages."[31] Bill Clinton had run his presidential campaign on a promise to "end welfare as we know it." With the implementation of the TANF program, he delivered on this promise. But the social welfare reformers in the 1990s failed to understand the direct impact accessible social welfare support had on protecting not only vulnerable mothers but also vulnerable children and, cumulatively, on keeping families together. By 2002, Black and Indigenous children had the highest rates of representation in the foster care system, at 17.4 and 14.1 per 1,000 children, respectively, compared to only 4.6 per 1,000 white children.[32]

The punitive social welfare policies that have defined the past three decades are designed on a model of shaming and punishing the families that the system claims to be helping. This attack, particularly on Black and Brown families, ties directly to societal assumptions about who is a good mother, who is bad, and who is not worthy of raising children. As historian Laura Briggs writes in *Taking Children: A History of American Terror*, throughout the 1990s and early 2000s, "Pregnancy became a more intense site of conflict."[33] Like a century ago, the most vulnerable women and mothers continue to be targeted as the root of many societal problems. And solutions continue to be in the form of taking away their children.

In the early 2000s, government policies began targeting immigrant and refugee families, many of whom had children who were born in the United States or had crossed the border as babies and small children. The family separation policies that evolved over the next three presidential administrations were a response to growing numbers of refugees, many of them families with small children, fleeing poverty and skyrocketing gang and domestic violence in Guatemala, Honduras, and El Salvador.[34] After the September 11, 2001, terrorist attacks, the George W. Bush administration began implementing comprehensive and intense crackdowns on immigrants and refugee seekers entering the United States.

Through Homeland Security initiatives, the Bush administration expanded family detention centers that facilitated family separation policies that would continue through the Obama, Trump, and Biden administrations. Workplace raids aimed at deporting undocumented immigrants and refugees resulted in the separation of thousands of children from their parents and family members. Children who were left behind in the United States after deportation raids were placed in foster-to-adopt social services without parental consent. Once parents and guardians were deported and children were placed in social service systems in the United States, it became nearly impossible for families to reunite. Children could not travel internationally without consent from parents or guardians, who were unable to provide consent from outside the country. More disturbing, "[s]tate child welfare systems often refused to work across national borders, and foster parents who were seeking to adopt often had little motivation—or simply lacked the knowledge—to find small children's parents."[35]

The Department of Health and Human Services (HHS) has worked in various capacities with the Department of Homeland Security over the past two decades in immigration practices that have facilitated family separation. And although there are instances of social workers refusing to participate in practices that many recognize as traumatizing and inhumane, there are also many instances of social workers who have actively and consciously facilitated child separation.[36]

The story of María Luis and her two young children is a heartbreaking example of the assumptions many case workers in social services made, and continue to make, about who is qualified to mother. In 2004, social workers were sent to Luis's home in Grand Island, Nebraska, on an anonymous tip to check on her two young children, whom she was home caring for while they were sick. Upon the workers' arrival at her home, frightened that her undocumented status would be revealed and her US-born children taken from her, Luis lied to them, saying she was the children's babysitter, not their mother. That same day she was arrested when the lie was revealed. Her two children, both US citizens, ages one and seven, were immediately put into protected services, and Luis was deported to Guatemala.

Luis would not see her children for four years as they floated through three different foster homes. She was finally able to return to the United States in 2008 for a court hearing, petitioning the court's decision to take her children from her. In 2009, the Nebraska Supreme Court reversed the earlier 2004 ruling on the grounds that Luis had not been given adequate rights to appeal the initial ruling that took her children from her. Luis had not been provided legal representation or an interpreter who could translate her first language, Quiché, an Indigenous Mayan dialect. In 2004, while her children were put into foster care and she was deported to Guatemala, Luis was left in the dark, not understanding what was happening to her children and what she could do about it. Social workers had failed to provide her with the information needed to regain custody of her children. The social workers involved testified that they believed Luis's children "would be better off staying in the United States."[37] Lastly, and most significantly, the 2009 court reversal found that the state failed to prove at any point that Luis was unfit to parent. Her children were taken from her because of her undocumented status and because, as the social workers testified, social services believed that other adults living in the United States would be better parents for Luis's children.

María Luis's horrific experience of nearly losing her children is not an outlier, just as Margaret Erle Katz's wasn't. We know the details of Luis's case because she fought against the system that delegitimized her right to mother her own children, and she won. The vast majority of mothers and families who continue to be separated from their children while or after they cross into the United States, seeking refuge and a better life for their children, do not have the enormous support that is needed to petition the courts to reverse family separation rulings. Immigrant and refugee parents and family members, like María Luis, are assessed by social services, immigration services, border control, and other government agencies as unassimilable and thus incapable of parenting. Their languages, cultures, and vulnerable situations of poverty disqualify them as legitimate parents.

Under the Trump administration's "zero tolerance" immigration policy, implemented in 2018, the Department of Justice began criminally prosecuting *all* people illegally entering the United States, regardless of any circumstances. Family separation was part and parcel of this policy, which in many ways lives on in the Biden administration.[38] In April 2022, Physicians for Human Rights published research from a clinical study of thirteen immigrant families that had been forcibly separated. All the family members in the study had some form of mental illness linked to the forced separation.[39]

The devastating impact of forced family separation and assimilation through adoption is well known to researchers, historians, Indigenous communities, and especially those who directly experienced the Indian adoption policies of the 1960s and 1970s (see chapter 2). Deborah Thibeault and Michael S. Spencer, researchers and professors of social work, published a scathing review in the *Social Service Review* in 2019 of the role social workers played during that period in taking Indigenous babies and children from their birth families and communities. They argue that changing the future of social work requires acknowledging past abuses and understanding how the social work profession has proliferated such abuses. The authors emphasize the importance of educating current social workers about historical instances of maltreatment and exploitation and the importance of social justice in family welfare practices. They don't mince words in their conclusion when they assert, "If social work education and the social work profession do not change their approach, oppression will not only continue; it will be perpetuated by a profession that claims to support vulnerable populations."[40]

Reflecting a similar philosophy of truth and reconciliation, in 2013, the Australian government issued a formal apology, given directly by Prime Minister Julia Gillard, for the government-sanctioned, decades-long practices of forcibly taking thousands of babies from unwed mothers. In her speech in the Great Hall of Parliament House in Canberra, Gillard proclaimed, "We deplore the shameful practices that denied you, the mothers, your fundamental rights and responsibilities to love and care for your children."[41] Currently, Belgium, Canada, Ireland, New Zealand, and the Netherlands have campaigns to issue similar, nationally recognized apologies for forced adoption practices.[42] The US government continues to separate families.

When we were kids, Rachel was the one who talked about being a mom when she grew up. She loved to dress and meticulously care for her dolls. In middle school, Rachel babysat the neighborhood kids, all of whom adored her. As a teenager, she gravitated toward babies and children, always knowing what to say to put a small kid at ease or how to confidently hold a baby so its head didn't flop around. Meanwhile, I was terrified and disgusted by babies and small children. At summer camp, I was chronically jealous of the youngest campers who would always flock to Rachel, following her and hanging on her every word like mini-groupies. She was the Pied Piper: kids always clamored to be in her presence. She loved kids, and they loved her.

I grew up certain that Rachel would thrive in motherhood, with the grace and ease she radiated when we were young, and I would be the one struggling to do it right. For a long time, I believe she felt this same confidence that someday she would be a great mom and walk a path her birth mother wasn't able to walk for her. By the time Rachel died, that confidence and dream had been decimated.

Several years after my sister gave her baby girl up for adoption, I became pregnant and prepared, for the first time in my life, to meet someone I was biologically connected to. I was ecstatic to be pregnant, but deep down, I was terrified. Would I fail like my sister had? Would I fail like my birth mother had? I needed support, especially from my sister, whom I spent my childhood believing I would emulate once I became a mom. Rachel also knew what it was like to be given up and face motherhood with all the uncertainty and fear that came with adoption.

The day before my baby shower, Rachel called me to tell me she wasn't coming. Our mom had asked all the baby shower guests to write a page of wisdom about mothering, which she then collected together in a book. When I asked Rachel if she would at least send a page for the book, she said, "Becca, you don't want a page from me. I have no advice to give. I'm a shit mom." My sister had lost custody of one child and then gave the second one away for adoption. I heard the sting of shame clearly in her voice that day when it stopped her from showing up for me at the start of my motherhood journey. She could not celebrate this journey I was on because, for her, that journey had ended in epic ignominy and grief.

There were layers of brutally difficult moments that compounded Rachel's final assessment of herself as a mother. Fertility and motherhood are challenging when your existence is defined by the shame of both. She was rarely validated as a mother by our family and community. Instead, it was her mistakes that came to define her journey as a mother. She walked the path alone, stumbling and struggling, and was never able to see herself or be seen as the mother she once believed she could be.

6

Reclaiming

The day we buried my sister in a small, quiet, and private burial service, my dearest and oldest friend gave birth to her only daughter. My best friend since kindergarten had wanted a child for years, and finally, at the age of forty-one, her dreams of motherhood came true. The night before my sister's burial, my friend struggled mightily in a long, painful, amazing home birth. I didn't sleep that entire night. My eyes were glued to my phone, waiting desperately for text updates from her husband and her mother. I needed that baby to come into this world almost as much as my dear friend's swollen, tired body needed it. The day we lowered my sister's coffin into the ground, my goddaughter was born. It was like a sweet, cool moment of relief amid a searing, exhausting pain that I just didn't think I could handle more of. As my family and I threw fistfuls of dirt on the coffin that housed my sister's bruised, cold body, this beautiful, pink, warm, shiny body emerged into our lives. Death followed by life is like the relief of warm sun after a cold, dark storm.

One week after the funeral, I flew to my friend's house to shop for groceries, clean the kitchen, switch loads of laundry, make meals, and, most importantly, hold this sweet, new baby girl. While my friend slept, still recovering from a long, exhausting labor, I held and rocked my baby goddaughter. And I talked to Rachel. I believe that in that transition after my sister's death and before my goddaughter's birth, the two met. They comforted each other as they prepared for their next journeys, one in death and one in life. In this way, my newborn goddaughter was my conduit to Rachel. While I walked my goddaughter around the yard, the warm sun shining on her tiny warm body, I told Rachel how much I missed her, how sorry I was for not listening to her. And, most important, for the first time, I told her that I finally understood that behind all her rage were deep pain and loneliness.

Until my sister's death, I believed she had abandoned me, choosing to burn through life on a wild roller coaster without regard for her family. But now I was swamped and choking on a sense of deep sadness and regret for not listening to Rachel. For the first time, I allowed myself to feel that same grief and anger my sister had in response to the circumstances of her own birth and adoption, and the adoption and loss of her own children. Rachel's birth, like mine, was silenced and erased. And now, in a vicious twist, Rachel was once again silenced in her death. Her death was shrouded in shame. So silenced was she in her death that for years to come, people close to her in life—friends from college, even her ex-husband—were never told she had died. Rachel's death was like an embarrassing secret, whispered about in hushed tones. During my quiet conversations walking around the yard with my newborn goddaughter, I knew I had to make Rachel's life matter. I had to end the silence.

In her memoir detailing her search for her birth family, Katrina Maxtone-Graham describes adoption as an "amputation from history."[1] To heal the wound of this amputation, the silence and lies that defined our lives, I had to reach out to those historical roots and threads and reattach them. History, the true stories of the past, became my way of speaking truth to power for Rachel now that she had lost her voice in death. History is constantly sticking its fingers into our present, everyday lives, whether or not we are aware of it. History has incredible power. It can paint pictures of where we came from and how the world and people in it looked, acted, and believed. This is weighty because how we understand ourselves and the world around us in this current moment is largely defined and shaped by what happened in the past. This is the power of historical narratives and historical memory. When people's lives in the past are silenced, this, in turn, silences people's lives in the present. But when these stories are told, it changes our understanding of the present world. When people's stories are shared, especially the lives of people who are deliberately traumatized and silenced, those awoken historical narratives directly affect the lives of people in the present. We start to view the world and our place in it differently, and then we actually start to *act* differently. And this, in turn, impacts the future. History is powerful.

There are brave, tenacious adoptees and activists who forged a path of telling the truth about adoption and demanding that America look at this history and change how adoption stories are told and, more important, how adoption transactions happen. Their actions over the past sixty-plus years have directly and profoundly affected how adoption in America unfolds today.

By the early 1970s, the period that marked the apex of domestic adoption in America, the societal narrative on adoption began to shift dramatically. The confluence of federally protected reproductive rights for women with the *Roe* decision of 1973, coupled with the growing acceptance of women raising children out of wedlock and the civil rights battles of Black and Indigenous activists who spoke out against the damaging impact of transracial and transnational adoption on children, all worked to push the narrative away from a decades-old pattern of forced and silenced relinquishment of babies. It is not a coincidence that the majority of these adoption reform activists were women. And it's not a coincidence that the narrative of adoption reform as a human rights issue finally began to take hold as a truth in the American psyche at the same time that women's rights to reproductive freedom were constitutionally recognized. Autonomy over one's fertility is inextricably linked to one's autonomy over one's parenthood. The womb and the person cannot be segregated.

At this same time, a new genre of both adoptee and birth mother memoir writing began hitting bookstore shelves. Search and reunion stories between adoptees and birth families were airing on national television. The American public became enthralled with this new genre of reality TV, where dramatic family reunions unfolded live on the screen. These stories exposed the personal, raw, and traumatic realities of adoption experiences. One of the most influential personal memoirs of this period, Florence Fischer's *The Search for Anna Fischer*, published in 1973, detailed Fischer's own search for her birth parents. The book landed on the *New York Times* best-seller list and became a how-to guide for many adoptees searching for their birth families.[2]

In tandem with writing her memoir, Fischer also founded the Adoptees' Liberty Movement Association (ALMA) in 1971. ALMA continues today as the largest and most comprehensive registry aimed at connecting adoptees to birth families.[3] In 1970, there were 89,000 domestic adoptions in the United States. By 1975, that number was down to 48,000.[4] The year I was born and adopted out, closed "stranger" adoptions—adoptions orchestrated secretly through private adoption agencies—were beginning to leave a bitter taste in the mouths of the American public.

The backstory of this shift in the American narrative on adoption had really started several decades earlier with the relentless work of an adoptee who presented American culture with a scathing critique of midcentury adoption practices, at a time when few people wanted to listen. In 1954, Jean Paton completed her first book about adoption, *The Adopted Break Silence*, succinctly summing up her mission to blow open both the silence and the shame around adoption in America. Her goal, a totally novel idea at the time, was to directly share the stories and feelings of adopted people surrounding adoption. Paton's opening line read, "Everyone except the adopted has been talking about adoption. About certain parts of adoption, the parts that can be seen and the parts that can be heard. The rest is silence—or was."[5]

Paton's book was the first social scientific piece of writing that directly centered adoptees' voices and experiences as authorities on adoption.[6] The direct and honest testimonies of adopted adults were narratives many Americans had never heard. One respondent in Paton's study explained,

> I would have preferred to have had parents who really wanted a child. My own parents never needed me, I was left in their hands. I am now forced to be grateful for something I never asked for and never wanted. I feel that children who are adopted should, since early age, be told of their adoption. They should also be told that they are wanted and loved. Affection makes a child feel secure. I don't think children should be adopted by wealthy people, not unless in extraordinary cases. The wealthier the parents, the more a child feels like a luxury toy, or the victim of people's wish to show off their "kindness."[7]

These personal narratives ran counter to what people believed and were told to believe about adoption: that it was an act of mercy and goodwill done for the betterment of the child.

Jean Paton's own adoption story was typical of adoption practices in the early 1900s. Her birth mother, Emma Cutting, was young and unmarried, and her working-class family made it clear that "a bastard child was not welcome in the Cutting home."[8] Jean's mother was sent away to a maternity home to wait out the pregnancy, give birth, and relinquish her baby. Two years after Jean was adopted by the first family, the Deans, her adoptive father died of cancer. Her adoptive mother couldn't afford to continue raising her, so she was transferred back to the Children's Home Society of Michigan. She stayed there for seven months and was then adopted by Thomas and Mary Paton. The Patons named her Jean. This would be her third name since birth.

With the Patons, Jean grew up in a privileged middle-class home. She loved her adoptive father dearly and would travel with him as he made medical house visits to his patients. Thomas and Mary Paton crafted a fanciful lie about Jean's birth parents, telling her, their neighbors, and their entire community that Jean's mother was from high Detroit society and her birth father was an accomplished musician in the city orchestra. This lie appeased Jean's questions about her origins for a while. And it shielded her adoptive parents from the encroaching shame they felt around adopting an illegitimate child and their own struggles with infertility.

When Jean entered college at Mount Holyoke in 1926, she faced social and academic hardships as she struggled to find answers about her identity. Seeing the impact of the lies he had told her about her birth family, Jean's father started a private search for her birth parents. As the search successfully progressed and Jean's father came close to finding her birth parents, he abruptly ended the search. Two decades later, Jean picked up where her father left off and managed quite easily to connect with her birth mother. But the decision on the part of her adoptive father to shut what she came to see as a vital door of connection profoundly alienated Jean from him.

This traumatic experience of coming so close to knowing the truth about her birth mother and birth community and then having it ripped away by her adoptive parent became a catalyst for her cause. Through her advocacy work over the next seventy years, the polestar of Paton's mission was to end the shame and silence around adoption. This manifested into the Life History Study Center, a registry connecting adoptees to birth families, and later her revolutionary adoptee support and search network, Orphan Voyage. Jean reappropriated the derogatory term "bastard," a term used to describe the societal failings of her own birth mother when she was pregnant with Jean in 1908. By the 1970s, Jean was declaring, "Bastards are beautiful!" in her writings and talks. This was two decades before adoptee activists Marley Greiner, Shea Grimm, and Damsel Plum created Bastard Nation in 1996, an organization whose singular and uncompromising aim is complete, unfettered access to all adoptee original birth records.[9]

By the time Jean Paton died in 2002 at the age of ninety-three, nearly all domestic adoptions in the United States espoused some form of openness between the adopting triad (birth parents, adoptee, and adopting family). Legal documents, including birth certificates, are no longer falsified or sealed away after birth.[10] Paton paved the way for centering and legitimizing voices speaking about adoption, especially the voices of adoptees. She was ahead of her time in this respect and in her call for making adoption rights a human rights issue.

In 1989, the United Nations ratified the UNCRC, which declared that children are not just objects who belong to their parents and for whom decisions are made, or adults in training. Rather, they are human beings and individuals in their own right.[11] The United States has signed the UNCRC but is the only UN member state that has not ratified it. Opposition to ratification most frequently comes from those who feel it would be too great of an imposition on parental rights. Unfortunately, this trope of defending parental rights, particularly in the context of the rights of adoptive parents, is the historical argument used to justify falsifying birth certificates, sealing adoption records, and silencing and shaming birth mothers. Activists like Paton and others had advocated for adoptee rights as human rights for decades, particularly as it related to babies and children taken from one family and literally sold to another under false pretenses and through the use of coercive and abusive practices. Paton's work, starting more than eighty years ago, would be one of the ripples to set a wave of change in motion.

Already by the 1970s, even when adoption records like mine were still being falsified and locked away, the national narrative was shifting. By 1975, the last year the federal government collected national data on domestic adoption, the number of transracial adoptions had dropped from 2,574, its peak in 1971, to 831.[12] During the 1960s, Black social workers had been tackling on a grassroots level the systemic racism in American culture sustained by the traditional mechanisms of the social work profession itself. Like Jean Paton, Black social workers during this time saw the horrors being perpetuated within their profession on a deep, critical level. As a young social worker in the 1940s, Paton had been instructed to arrange the surrender of infants by birth mothers.[13] Those early, gut-wrenching experiences would become a catalyst for Paton to leave the field of social work altogether and focus all her energy on reversing that destructive work, creating unification where families had been severed. Two decades later, Black social workers went a significant step further by demanding that the profession itself own its destructive policies and change.

At the 1969 NASW annual conference, the national body of Black social workers did not mince words when it declared, "The NASW has been, and is now, irrelevant to meeting the needs of Black people. We feel that the NASW is not committed to system changes in the interest of Black folk." One of the fundamental demands in its statement was that white people confront their own racist attitudes and actions and that "Black Experts (not white experts who heretofore acted as experts) speak to the issues confronting the Black community."[14]

The NABSW's direct and effective advocacy against transracial adoption, specifically the transfer of Black babies into white homes, would become one of the organization's best-known battles against systemic and abusive racism in America. In 1972, a year after the peak in transracial domestic adoption in America, the NABSW issued a public statement denouncing transracial adoption, identifying it as a form of racial and cultural genocide. The statement read, "We fully recognize the phenomenon of transracial adoption as an expedient for white folk, not as an altruistic human concern for black children. The supply of white children for adoption has all but vanished and adoption agencies, having always catered to middle class whites, developed an answer to their desire for parenthood by motivating them to consider black children."[15] The NABSW forced the nation to look beyond the needs of the adoptive family by exposing the destructive bigotry operating within adoption practices. The organization fully understood that behind racist adoption policies and the long history of eugenics-inspired sterilization policies was a societal distrust and disdain for Black mothers. The call for transferred authority to Black experts included a shift of authority to Black women social workers and doctors who were also mothers.

Part of this strategy included a shifting focus of care onto broader communities connected to the child, including birth communities. Black family preservation was a cornerstone of the NABSW's 1972 declaration against transracial adoption. As the organization emphasized, when Black children were taken out of Black communities and placed into white homes, they were "cut off from the healthy development of themselves as Black people."[16] Decades later, this statement would be reflected in the United Nations International Children's Emergency Fund's (UNICEF) 2007 press release on adoption:

Adoption should always be the last resort for the child. The CRC [Committee on the Rights of the Child], which guides UNICEF's work, states very clearly that every child has the right to know and to be cared for by his or her own parents, whenever possible. UNICEF believes that families needing support to care for their children should receive it, and that alternative means of caring for a child should only be considered when, despite this assistance, a child's family is unavailable, unable or unwilling to care for her or him.[17]

The work of the NABSW pushed the nation a step closer to acknowledging not only adoptee rights as human rights but also birth family rights as human rights. In situations where keeping birth families together was impossible, the NABSW turned its words into direct action by creating adoption assistance programs specifically for Black families. It also aided in the growth of Black-run adoption agencies and lobbied for the creation of subsidized adoptions for Black families.[18]

Seven years after the NABSW issued its public statement in opposition to transracial adoption and were developing fundamental changes in social work practices that centered on support for Black birth mothers and Black communities, a woman by the name of Lee Campbell appeared on the nationally televised, hugely popular *Phil Donahue Show*. In front of millions of Americans, Lee Campbell sat alone at the center of a studio stage and bravely shared her experience of being forced to give up her baby for adoption. Campbell recounted that she was seventeen years old, still in high school, and totally powerless against her parents' and her boyfriend's parents' decisions about what would happen to her body and her baby. As she described the details of her forced relinquishment, she explained, "I was the oldest of five and we had to protect my four younger siblings. My younger brother was in fights on the streets to protect my good name. Friends of my sisters were not allowed to hang around with my sisters because of the contagion of the hereditary lack of morality."[19] Campbell went on to unpack in detail the societal shame thrust upon her the minute she got pregnant and the unraveling of support and community that followed. The saving grace of Campell's experience of being sent off to an out-of-state birthing home to give birth to her baby boy and then relinquish him was that she was permitted by the nurses to hold her baby, and to nurse and care for him before he was taken from her and given away. Sixteen years after the birth of her son, two years before she was featured on *Donahue*, Campbell reconnected with her son. With the support of his adoptive family, they established a lifelong relationship.

In 1976, the year after I was born, Lee Campbell founded CUB to support birth parents who had lost children to adoption. Through her work, Campbell would talk with thousands of birth parents, documenting the psychological impact of parent-child separation through adoption.[20] Testifying to the intense trauma endured particularly by birth parents who weren't given the right to hold and connect with their babies before relinquishment, Campbell stated on *Donahue*, "Those birthparents who come to CUB who have seen their children, who have held their children, they are better than those who do not."[21]

Campbell lifted the veil on the devastating effects on birth mothers of both forced relinquishment and the societal shame and silence that permeated pregnancies and relinquishment scenarios. At a time when the societal narrative still depicted birth mothers as, in Campbell's words, "contagion[s] of the hereditary lack of morality," Campbell shifted the blame away from birth mothers and back toward society. In the televised *Donahue Show*, which aired in millions of American living rooms, Campbell forced the nation to see her humanity as a birth mother who had endured incredible trauma through the forced relinquishment of her baby.

The family unification work of countless adoption activists and organizations, coupled with the amplification of voices of people traumatized through inhumane adoption practices, has brought our nation to a place where silenced and sealed adoption transactions are extremely rare in domestic adoptions. And most domestic adoption agencies actively discourage a closed adoption policy. By the end of the twentieth century, domestic adoption policies in both the public and the private sector had transformed into a system in which birth mothers had substantial rights to choose who adopted their babies and to contact and communicate with adoptive parents.

Today domestic adoption rights battles in the United States focus on retroactively unsealing adoption records so that those who were adopted out years ago under old policies of concealment can finally know the truth of their identities.[22] Currently, only eleven states in the country allow adoptees complete and unfettered access to their original birth certificates.[23] The remaining states require adult adoptees to run a gauntlet of restrictive obstacles including steep processing fees, mutual consent from an adoption registry, or even a court order, as is my case with the state of California. For most adopted people born before 1990, during the time when birth records were regularly falsified and sealed, it remains very challenging to find the truth of our identities. Continued claims against unsealing birth records rest on an argument for protecting the identities of birth parents. State records collected between 2004 and 2014 show that during that decade, 1,760 adoptees requested original birth records across the nation. Only thirteen birth parents submitted forms saying they didn't want to be contacted.[24]

The birth parent protection argument conflicts with adoption rights advocacy pursued over the past sixty years by organizations like CUB, whose retributive work exposes the desire for connection and healing on both sides of the transaction. Catholic organizations have argued that opening adoption records would increase the likelihood of women seeking abortions.[25] In 2015, the Pennsylvania Catholic Conference made this argument in its testimony against state House Bill 162, which would have given adoptees unfettered access to their original birth records.[26] Adoption rights and reproductive rights continue to be intricately intertwined. Illinois state representative Sara Feigenholtz, an adoptee who sponsored a similar bill in the Illinois House of Representatives in 2010 that would allow for easier access to birth records, succinctly summarized the insincerity of the antiabortion, anti–open records argument when she argued, "Women don't get pregnant and say, 'I'm going to have an abortion because this person may find me.' It's almost an insult to women."[27]

The potency of family reunification and the truth-telling that emerges through these experiences has been a powerful theme in adoption reform over the past two decades. This theme is especially emblematic in the activism of Sandy White Hawk. In the early 2000s, White Hawk, a Sicangu Lakota adoptee and survivor of mid-twentieth-century Indian adoption policies, would come onto the adoption reform scene and have a monumental impact on how adoption is talked about and practiced in Indigenous communities across the United States and Canada.

In the summer of 1999, Sandy White Hawk attended the Rosebud Fair, the celebration of the Rosebud Lakota Sioux held annually on the Rosebud, South Dakota, fairgrounds. The multiday celebration includes a rodeo, Little League tournaments, garden contests, and most important, the powwow. The nearly 150-year-old tradition is a celebration "that literally serves as an essential conduit in the continued exercise of our Lakota traditions and culture from one generation to the next."[28] White Hawk recounts watching a typical "special" where time is taken out to honor someone. The powwow dancing stops, and everyone watches and listens to the person speaking about the honoree. The person being honored was a Korean War veteran. White Hawk watched as the family walked to the slow honor beats and made their way around the arena alone before powwow participants came out to shake his hand and then fall in behind the family. This homecoming was an essential piece of healing the veteran's war traumas, a reconnection to home and community. In watching this special, something struck White Hawk. She had never seen or heard of a song or special that "welcomed adoptees back to the circle."[29] White Hawk knew personally what that separation from home, from community, from ancestors felt like.

When she was just eighteen months old, White Hawk was removed from her Sicangu Lakota family and adopted by a white missionary couple who had moved from Illinois to "work with the Indians."[30] After they adopted White Hawk, they moved to rural Wisconsin. She was raised far from the Rosebud Reservation, first on a farm after her adoptive father's death, then to a small town of approximately four thousand people, where she was the only Indigenous girl. As she recalls, "It was very difficult growing up in a town where my image wasn't reflected in any way."[31]

As a child, White Hawk was told by her adoptive mother that her birth mother gave her up because she didn't want her, that she kept her at birth only so that she could get a welfare check and drink. White Hawk suffered abuse in her adoptive home and grew up feeling ugly, alone, and unworthy of love. She knew this narrative of flat-out rejection from her birth community was not the comprehensive truth about her adoption. When White Hawk was thirty-four years old, she traveled back to the Rosebud Reservation for the first time since her adoption. It felt like coming home. By then, her birth mother had died, but White Hawk connected with her brother, her sister, her uncles, and the greater Rosebud Sioux tribal community.

At the Rosebud Fair, White Hawk saw what a powwow could offer adoptees like herself who had been taken far from their tribal communities as babies and young children. "Adoptees had never heard, 'Welcome Home,' and I wanted that for them."[32] White Hawk kept these thoughts to herself until she met Chris Leith. Leith was a Prairie Island Dakota elder and spiritual advisor and, at the time, was the Spiritual Advisor to the National Indian Child Welfare Association. When she met Leith, White Hawk was a Native American student advisor at Madison Area Technical College, and she asked him to come speak with students.[33] Before class, White Hawk and Leith sat down to talk and eat breakfast together. In that casual and intimate moment, Leith asked White Hawk if she had gone to the Rosebud Fair. She shared with

Leith her experiences and thoughts from the fair and the opportunity she saw for calling home adoptees. Upon hearing this, Leith stopped eating and said, "You're right. There should be a song. I'll make sure there's a song. I'll ask Jerry Dearly to make a song."[34]

The floodgates opened, and from there, Sandy White Hawk, in collaboration with Chris Leith and other tribal elders, community leaders, and activists, was invited to Indian communities and Canada to share their developing work on addressing the grief and loss caused by separation from family and community. This work and White Hawk's mission of creating family reconnection for Indigenous adoptees evolved into her creation of the First Nations Repatriation Institute (FNRI). Through the FNRI, White Hawk is working to close the circle of work started by the courageous and tenacious Indigenous mothers and activists who fought for the passage of the ICWA in 1978, women who had witnessed firsthand the literal forced removal of babies and children from their birth families and tribal communities. The purpose of the ICWA continues to be to "protect the best interests of Indian children and to promote the stability and security of Indian tribes and families by the establishment of minimum Federal standards for the removal of Indian children from their families and the placement of such children in foster or adoptive homes which will reflect the unique values of Indian culture, and by providing for assistance to Indian tribes in the operation of child and family service programs."[35] With the passage of the ICWA, tribal courts, not states, have the authority to protect Indigenous children and stop the unwarranted removal of children from their homes, families, and communities. Family preservation is a foremost goal of the policy.

Nationwide, Indigenous children remain three times more likely than white children to be placed in foster care. In South Dakota, they are ten times more likely to be placed in foster care. And in Minnesota, they are twenty-two times more likely.[36] In many ways, the vision of the ICWA has yet to be realized. Indigenous babies and children are still being taken from their birth homes and communities at a horrifying rate. The work of the FNRI is prescient and desperately needed.

One of the most dominant criticisms of the ICWA as a policy is that, in limiting the fostering and adoption of Indigenous babies and children into non-Indigenous homes, the policy is racially motivated. This "color-blind" critique of the ICWA depends on the idea that Indigenous peoples are simply a different race. This fosters a belief by non-Native adopting families that by raising Indigenous babies in non-Native cultures, the children can fluidly assimilate, shedding their ancestral identity. In reality, tribal sovereignty means acknowledging the different, diverse tribal nations and communities, each with vastly different languages, cultures, traditions, and histories. The adoption of Indigenous children into non-Native homes and communities means that those children do not grow up understanding where they come from and who they are. Sandy White Hawk's work with the FNRI involves reweaving those deep, powerful threads of connection between adoptees and their culture, tribal history, language, and community. The painful stories told by the Indigenous adoptees White Hawk works with demonstrate the devastating impact this severing from tribal ancestry and community has on individuals who are raised not knowing their past.

The two wings of White Hawk's work with the FNRI exhibit the organization's ability to both reach back to heal the traumas of the past and reach forward to change foster and adoption practices in the future. White Hawk facilitates healing circles for Indigenous adoptees wrenched by separation from their families and community. Compared to white adoptees in the United States, Indigenous adoptees are more likely to experience "alcohol addiction, drug addiction, drug recovery, self-assessed eating disorder, eating disorder diagnosis, self-injury, suicidal ideation, and suicide attempt."[37]

Adoption trauma for Indigenous adoptees is compounded by the intergenerational trauma from genocide, forced removal from tribal lands and communities, and cultural assimilation in US government Indian boarding schools. Through dialogue and listening in a supportive space, adoptees can share their lived experiences and, for many, speak to the liminal space they have lived in as neither Native nor white. The space of dialogue and healing that White Hawk has helped create in Native communities has been not only a conduit for adoptees to share their stories but also a space for survivors of Indian boarding schools to share their experiences of forced assimilation, including White Hawk's brother Leonard, who attended the Rosebud Boarding School in Mission, South Dakota.

The act of simply speaking about their experiences and giving voice to the years of pain endured through silence facilitates profound healing for adoptees. Like Jean Paton's early work of centering the voices of adoptees as vital authorities on adoption in *The Adopted Break Silence*, and Lee Campbell's work giving rise to the voices of birth mothers, White Hawk's healing work centers on amplifying adoption experiences directly through the words of adoptees. When White Hawk first began this journey of creating a space for Native adoptees to come home and shared her ideas with Chris Leith, he imparted to her the wisdom he had leaned on for years as a tribal elder and spiritual leader. He said, "Pray with your heart, not your head."[38] The practice of speaking of one's felt experience with adoption into a community and then being held and called in by that community is a profound, heartfelt experience.

The forward-reaching wing of the FNRI's work involves education, particularly in the field of social work. White Hawk facilitates training for lawyers, guardians ad litem, mental health workers, judges, and social workers across the country. A pivotal part of this education involves teaching people the history of trauma and disenfranchisement from US government Indian policy in both assimilation through education and assimilation through adoption policies. The full circle of healing from the past and changing the future is best summarized by White Hawk: "Our families are still in that place of healing. As adoptees share their stories it encourages everyone to share what happened to them as well."[39]

When White Hawk talks with fully licensed social workers in educational settings, she shares her personal experience with the Indian adoption policies of the 1950s that facilitated removing Indigenous children from birth communities instead of assisting Indigenous communities and Indigenous birth mothers with resources and support. In this way, one of the key educational goals of the FNRI is to transform the field of social work so that its practitioners have a deeper understanding of the families that come to them for service, knowing that these families are in crisis and need to be treated with humanity.[40] Family separation, rooted in dogmatic assumptions about Indigenous communities and Indigenous parenting, compounds trauma on a multigenerational level.

Like the NABSW in the 1970s and 1980s, the FNRI is working to reform social services and adoption practices from the inside out and the ground up. The impact of this approach of both healing from the past and transforming the future changes how we all understand and talk about adoption. White Hawk shares her own experience of healing: "In telling it and re-telling it [her adoption story] it helped me remove the shame."[41] Amplifying the voices of those who have suffered and been silenced in the adoption and assimilation process has the power to change the future.

As domestic adoption policies in the United States progressively became more open in the past twenty years and spaces for family reunification, like those created by the FNRI, shifted a narrative toward family healing, an opposite trend of silencing and abuse proliferated in transnational adoption practices until their apex in 2005.[42] Part of what fueled that shift toward transnational adoption and away from domestic adoption in the 1980s and 1990s was the move toward open adoption policies in domestic adoption transactions within the United States.[43] Many adopting parents saw the now nearly mandatory connection to birth mothers and birth communities as threatening. Less regulated transnational adoption agencies allowed adopting families a clean break from any birth family or community ties. Through transnational adoptions, adopting parents could completely avoid any interaction with or connection to their adopted child's birth mother or, even more disturbingly, the truth behind the relinquishment of the child.

As highlighted in chapter 3, transnational adoption practices historically and currently demonstrate the toll adoption has on children and birth communities when it is run as a business. Today's multimillion-dollar transnational adoption industry still depends on both the commodification of children and the dehumanization of birth mothers and birth communities. Through secrecy and unregulated, abusive practices in the transnational adoption industry, the fertility of women living outside the United States becomes a valued commodity, especially as the supply of adoptable babies and children stateside diminishes.

In 2009, investigative journalist E. J. Graff coauthored an op-ed in the *New York Times* titled "Celebrity Adoptions and the Real World." The provocative article, highlighting the transnational adoptions by Madonna and Angelina Jolie, succinctly and powerfully summarized the ethical and moral issues plaguing transnational adoption. Graff and her coauthors pointed out the incredible needs of millions of children around the world living on the streets and in orphanages. But they also uncovered the duplicity of a system that claims to provide an antidote to these inhuman living conditions of millions of children, especially by peeling back the fictitious façade that all these children are abandoned, orphaned, or have no connection to any community that actively wants to care for them:

> In trying to adopt Mercy James, Madonna's intention might be humanitarian: she may hope to save a child from institutional misery and loneliness. It might be selfish: she wants a child to love. It might be a self-justifying mixture of both. But in trying to adopt a child who already has a family, Madonna is inadvertently exposing the seamier underside of international adoption: the fact that, too often, the amounts of money that Western adoption agencies spend in poor countries is helping to defraud, coerce or kidnap children away from families that wanted to raise them to adulthood.[44]

The family of the child Madonna adopted from Malawi demanded her custody prior to the transnational adoption, and organizations including Save the Children and UNICEF both called for a denial of Madonna's adoption requests and the general abatement of the transnational adoption on the grounds that family separation must be allowed only as an absolute last resort. The adoption still went through. In the conclusion of the *NYT* op-ed, the coauthors called for a shift of monetary and social policy focus *away* from transferring children out of their impoverished homes and sending them thousands of miles away, and *toward* a focus on providing support for those families and communities in places like Malawi so that they could raise their own children with access to clean water, vaccinations, and schools *within* their birth communities and families.

The research of legal scholar and coauthor of the *NYT* op-ed David Smolin on transnational adoption exposed the deep corruption that facilitated the trafficking, kidnapping, and stealing of babies and children for adoption, as well as the devastating forces that facilitated the commodification of babies and children in a market where American families could pay upward of $52,000 per child.[45] In a scathing report published in the *Wayne Law Review* in 2006, Smolin didn't mince words when he wrote, "Child laundering reduces the humanitarian rationale for inter-country adoption into a cruel façade or pretext. Stripped of all humanitarian justification, intercountry adoption is a commercialized and corrupt system driven by the demand of rich Western adults for children. Thus, if child laundering is present to a significant degree within the intercountry adoption system, as this article claims, then the ethical and legal legitimacy of intercountry adoption is threatened."[46]

Smolin's astounding work uncovering corruption and abuse in the transnational adoption market has been featured on National Public Radio, ABC News, Al Jazeera, and CBC Radio and in the *New York Times* and the Hague Special Commission on the Practical Operation of the Hague Adoption Convention. In addition, his work has had a significant impact on the trajectory of transnational adoption in America. Since 2005, transnational adoptions in the United States have been on a precipitous decline, as corrupt, child-trafficking, and horrifically inhuman practices have been exposed. In 2004, at the apex of transnational adoptions, 22,989 adoptees came into the United States. By 2017, that number was down to 4,714 adoptions, the lowest since 1973.[47]

Contributing to this growing awareness of the inhuman practices that have come to define transnational adoption are the voices of transnational adoptees and birth mothers who, through creative outlets, have found ways to voice their experiences and shed light on the traumas they have endured. Organizations like Intercountry Adoptee Voices and Adopted Vietnamese International have provided platforms for transnational adoptees to share their stories in a supportive community. As with the powerful impact that storytelling has had on Indigenous adoptees who connect through the FNRI, the collective sharing of heartfelt stories of transnational adoptees has created a wave of change in transnational adoption practices.

These foundational changes, many of them ongoing, reflect the work of incredibly brave individuals who have come forward to speak their truth and share their stories. David Smolin's journey exposing the inhumanity and abuse in transnational adoption began with his own adoption story and the brave steps he and his family took to expose the truth. David and his wife, Desiree, adopted two girls, Manjula and Bhagya, from India in 1998. They went through a reputable, experienced US adoption agency that told them the girls were orphaned and had been waiting a long time for a home. David and Desiree would quickly learn, on the insistence of the girls themselves once they arrived in the United States, that they had been kidnapped.

The Smolins began a journey first of reuniting their adopted daughters with their birth mother and then sharing their story with NPR and countless other platforms with the aim of ending child abduction through adoption.[48] Manjula and Bhagya's birth mother had been told that her daughters, taken from her because of her poverty, would be placed temporarily in a boarding school in India. In reality, they were trafficked into adoption and eventually sent to the Smolins in Atlanta, Georgia.

The truth behind Manjula and Bhagya's experience and the especially devastating experience of their birth mother, whose girls were literally stolen from her, is a sharp contrast to the feel-good stories marketed by adoption agencies. By prioritizing the reunification of Manjula and Bhagya's birth mother with her stolen daughters, the Smolins validated her human right to parenthood. And by demanding truth and reconciliation, the Smolins have been part of a larger healing process that begins with the truth. As Sandy White Hawk shared from her own experience of healing, the act of telling her story helped remove the shame.[49]

A week before my sister's funeral, I got the final addition to the tattoo on my inner ankle. Swimming off the end of the makau, with its long tail unwrapping from the hook's handle, is now a Polynesian-style manta ray. When my husband first met my sister, the year after we returned from our voyage sailing around the world, he affectionately called her Ray Ray, his nickname for Rachel. Rachel loved it. She loved my husband, with his "Fuck 'em if they can't take a joke" attitude. He was unconventional and unapologetic in who he was, and my sister thought he was a riot and the exact opposite of the stuffed-up, arrogant, conformist guy she thought I would marry. Having my sister's informal blessing that I had picked a good guy, a good partner, meant the world to me. And from then on, we both lovingly referred to my sister as Ray Ray.

In the winter of 2017, in the months leading up to Rachel's death, the blockbuster Disney film *Moana* hit movie theaters across America. My daughters were six and eight years old. The film was the center of their universe. Within the first few months of the film's release, we must have watched it at least ten times as a family. I loved it because my girls loved it. But I also felt a personal connection to this story of a girl who is called to the water, gets on a boat, and sails across the ocean to find answers about her ancestors. Moana's courage and vulnerability were riveting for me. The most captivating scene of the movie was when Moana's grandmother's spirit, as a glorious, iridescent manta ray, comes to guide her when she is alone and desperate, lost at sea. Moana's grandma ascends upon her boat in her human form, smiles, and says, "Guess I chose the right tattoo," glancing over her shoulder at the manta ray tattoo covering her upper back. She then encourages Moana to follow her heart, offering her love and support unconditionally by singing, "Sometimes the world seems against you. / The journey may leave a scar. / But scars can heal and reveal just / where you are." Every time this scene came on the screen, I would sit in my seat in the movie theater weeping and weeping. I so desperately needed that grandma when I felt alone at sea.

When Rachel died, I remembered that scene in the movie. The grandma's manta ray spirit circling Moana's boat in the dark water played over and over in my head while I sat in my car, stood in line at the grocery store, and waited to pick my kids up at summer camp, with hot tears rolling down my swollen cheeks. The manta ray in Polynesian tattoo art is considered a symbol of protection, as a spirit guide against danger. This comes from the ray's ability to hide from prey by lying still and peacefully under the sand. The Hawaiian name for manta ray is *hāhālua*, which translates to "two mouths" or "two breaths." Through the course of their lives, the great manta rays can journey across huge parts of the world's oceans. Their ability to navigate ocean depths, evade prey, and appear to be flying as they swoop and dive to eat with their two wide mouths gives them the aura of both power and grace. The moment Rachel died I knew I had to mark my body one final time. And now, a week before the funeral, I knew that a manta ray was meant to be that final piece of my tattoo. Ray Ray was now my spirit guide.

7

Rebirth

Becoming is the action that births our womanhood,
rather than the passive act of being born (an act none
of us has a choice in). This short, powerful statement
assured me that I have the freedom, in spite of and
because of my birth, body, race, gender expectations,
and economic resources, to define myself for myself
and for others.

Janet Mock

One of the ancient wonders of the world is the Lighthouse of
Alexandria. Built by the Ptolemaic Kingdom during the reign
of Ptolemy II Philadelphus between 280 and 247 BCE, the
lighthouse stood roughly one hundred meters tall and was, in
its time and for centuries to come, one of the tallest human-
made structures on the planet. Standing on the western edge of
the Nile Delta, this light beacon guided vessels coming in and
out of the port of Alexandria, one of the pinnacle locations of
maritime trading traffic in the ancient world. It is prescient that
a lighthouse would be considered a wonder of the world. As an
experienced sailor and someone who has lived at sea for long
periods, I see lighthouses as symbolic in their ability to speak
truth and guide people.

The point of the lighthouse is to signify shallow water and hazards therein, particularly rocks. Lighthouses alert you to danger but also allow you, in knowing the danger, to make calculated decisions and thus continue to adventure. In this sense, they provide freedom. They are guides. They don't lie. They speak the truth, no bullshit, a bright light in the night and a visibly coded tower seen in the day. And they emit a coded horn when visibility is low, so you can hear them even when you can't see them. You see them and hear them if you choose to look and listen. And if you choose not to listen or see, you do it at your own peril. Lighthouses are truth-tellers. And they tell you what is underneath, what most of us cannot see but can destroy us.

When you are at sea, the shore becomes incredibly dangerous. This is somewhat duplicitous because you must come ashore; and as anyone who has spent long periods out at sea can attest, you hit a point where you really, really crave coming ashore. Yet doing so is often a dangerous and strategic exercise. Open water provides sailors a level of safety because of the draft of the ship. Being in deep, offshore waters means you don't have to worry about running aground or smashing into anything. Depth becomes a frenetic focus, especially as you near shore. Shallow water is treacherous. As the ground beneath your ship rises, unseen, it threatens to rip apart your vessel. And so you rely on a guide to safely steer you to shore. When I boarded a ship in the fall after graduating from college, I began a journey that would bring into my life women, ship mothers, who, like lighthouses, would speak truth to power and guide me.

In my senior year of college, I began to consciously ponder the idea of searching for my birth mother, my people. This was a pivotal point in my life. I was leaving the safety and security of college and now had to really invent myself as an adult. And this got me thinking, for the first time in a conscious way, about what it would take to search for my biological family and, even more significant, what it might be like to actually find them. So I started on a search journey, with the beginning steps of asking my parents for what little information might exist and possibly contacting a private investigator for help. My parents told me, as they had so many times before, that my adoption was done in secret, my birth mother gave an alias, all communication was done through a lawyer, they had no idea who she was, and it would be nearly impossible to find her. In closing, my parents said she didn't want to be found. By sharing that they would help yet claiming it was futile, they simultaneously opened a door and shut it.

As the birth family search was evolving into a nearly impossible endeavor, the only next move at my disposal was attempting to file a court order to open my sealed birth documents, which was a long shot. I felt hopeless. And then an opportunity for a different journey presented itself to me, and I walked away from the birth mother search, or so I thought. I discovered a ship. While visiting some friends one weekend in Woods Hole, Massachusetts, I found a pamphlet on my windshield advertising a sailing training ship that would soon set off on a global circumnavigation. Two months later, I flew to Nova Scotia, where I joined the crew of a three-masted, traditionally rigged tall ship and spent the next two years of my life sailing around the world. I remember with great clarity that, when I signed on for this sailing adventure, I decided to table my search for my birth mother. At the time, walking onto this ship meant walking away from this mother search. But it turned out to be a walk toward a different type of mother search.

Our slow-moving home for this two-year global voyage was a 180-foot, three-masted barque. This meant that the sails on the forward two masts were square-rigged, like those big, square-shaped sails running perpendicular to the ship that you see in pirate movies. Like a scene out of *Pirates of the Caribbean*, the ship was exquisite to see, especially from a distance, like something rising up over the horizon from out of time. But up close, on deck and down below, exquisite elegance and beauty were replaced with the real and jarring sights, textures, and smells of life on board a traditional sailing ship. The term "traditional" did not just apply to the rig of the ship. The living quarters and resources available to us in our daily lives were much as they were for nineteenth- and early-twentieth-century sailors. The majority of the crew slept in large communal sleeping spaces. Each person's only place of privacy consisted of a bunk not much larger than a tall coffin, with a thin curtain drawn separating you from the twenty other people sleeping in the same space. In the tropics, where we spent most of our journey, the heat and humidity, especially belowdecks and in the bunks, were stifling. The cooking was all done on a large coal stove in the tiny galley, which was even more stifling than the bunks unless a good breeze was blowing. Laundry was done by hand in buckets, and it's an exaggeration to say that once we'd hand-washed and line-dried our laundry on deck, it was any cleaner than when we'd started.

Our three modern luxuries on board consisted of a water desalination system that allowed us to produce abundant amounts of drinkable water filtered from seawater, three large freezers in the cargo hold that allowed for a somewhat improved diet on long ocean passages, and two flushable toilets. Our life on deck and on watch fell into a predictable rhythm most of the time. We lived by a naval watch system, working three-part shifts over a twenty-four-hour day, meaning we worked four hours and then had eight hours off to rest, eat, and sleep. My watch, which consisted of a captain's mate who ran the watch and about eight other sailors, worked the four-to-eight shift. We were on duty cleaning, repairing the rig, painting, sanding, and manning sails—all work that was continuous and endless—every day from 4 A.M. to 8 A.M. and then again from 4 P.M. to 8 P.M. I would spend the next two years of my life following this routine, living this rhythm, which, at times of calm seas, was incredibly monotonous and both mind-numbingly dull and phenomenally peaceful. At other times, in extreme weather, when all daily jobs ceased and everyone had to work the sails with speed and precision to get through a storm, it was the most exhilarating and terrifying experience of my life.

Patterns emerge in these intense and isolated living experiences that become totally normal and accepted, yet, once you leave that unique space, you realize their insanity. A ship runs, thrives, and really can survive only with order and structure. This can be said for all circumstances of life, but on a ship out at sea, when life becomes expressly vulnerable, this is especially true. Rules become everything on a ship; following those rules is not optional. Some of the most basic rules that defined our life on the ship included:

- Repeat orders back to those giving commands.
- Don't talk about work at mealtime.
- Don't be a slacker—this means "mill about smartly," or always look like you are ready to work even if you aren't working.
- Bravery is determined by your willingness and ability to work up in the rig (high above the deck).
- Walk softly on deck as there was always someone sleeping, even in the middle of the day.
- Come back from off-watch shore time with a good story or adventure to tell.
- Be as masculine as possible—traditional femininity is a weakness.

The ship's crew included many incredibly strong, brave, and competent women. Our second mate, the person who was third in command of the entire ship, was a woman. Our ship's doctor was a woman. Our second engineer was a woman. And there were among us amazingly talented women who, before the journey, had established careers in law, film, science, and publishing. As women on the ship, stuck in a system plucked directly out of the nineteenth century when women were shunned from working in any capacity on ships—when the mere presence of a woman on a ship was considered incredibly bad luck—our status depended on being tough, nonemotional, calculated, and skillful in navigation and the trade of seamen. We had to be willing to get our hands dirty, take physical risks, and demonstrate physical strength—all with a look of indifference on our faces. To pass as a sailor, even in the late twentieth century, you had to act like a man. Things are changing, but in 1997, it was a paradox being a woman and a sailor on a traditionally rigged ship. And all the women, especially the women leaders on the ship, had to navigate this paradox with deft strategy. It required redefining what it meant to be a sailor, allowing women into that identity without compromising all the revered traits of a sailor: strong, brave, hardworking, competent, yet eager for adventure. All of these characteristics had to be wrapped in an aura of nonchalance. Emotion, vulnerability, and honesty did not hold a place in this space.

While I was on the ship, this kind of traditional, hypermasculine identity was not openly tested. But on a daily basis, in subtle ways, it was indirectly challenged. The women leaders on the ship dexterously navigated this paradoxical identity of sailor and woman in subversive ways. There were multiple times on board when the second mate made calculated decisions about where we would anchor, what we would set for sails. She made navigational decisions that flew directly in the face of those made by the captain—decisions that would prove to be beneficial and, in some cases, pivotal in creating safety and security for the crew. It was the women on the ship who would bring people together in several moments of crisis, when the entire journey was in jeopardy. At one point, when over half the crew considered abandoning the voyage because of unbearable living conditions and frustrations with the captain's leadership, these women rallied the crew, telling them not to suck it up and trudge ahead but to speak the truth, call out the bullshit that was making the voyage insufferable, and force a change so that the voyage could continue.

These women became the lighthouses on our journey around the world. They saw what was unfolding clearly when leaders were abusive, and when unsafe and ego-driven decisions were being made. And they shined a light on these rocks that threatened the voyage. As truth-tellers, they called out hypocrisies and incongruencies that existed in our lives on the ship. And after the trip, they were collectively recognized as the great leaders who held things together and made the journey possible.

As a young woman living my first stage of life as a real adult, and in this insane, tumultuous world on a ship in the middle of the ocean, thousands of miles from home, I desperately looked to these women for guidance at every turn. They were all older, wiser, stronger, and more resilient than me. I clung to them like a toddler clinging desperately to her mother's hand as they walked through a wild, scary forest full of shadows, light, monsters, and magical creatures. They became my mothers in ways that my adoptive mother never could. They guided and led with inner strength, honesty, and vulnerability instead of shame and fear. They created safe spaces on the ship and challenged the notion that you couldn't be brave and vulnerable at the same time. They encouraged crew members to take risks, not by pushing them off the ledge but by building up their confidence and drive to thrive so that they *chose* to jump off the ledge. Through their leadership, they became the ship mothers. These were the mothers I wanted to emulate.

I joined the ship thinking I was walking away from a search for my birth mother, and I came away from the journey two years later with many mothers. And most of these ship mothers, these lighthouses, would never have children. They would never grow babies in their bellies or raise children. But they mothered as leaders. And most importantly, they challenged not just what it meant to be a sailor but what it meant to be a mother *and* a leader. I walked off the ship, my home for two years, and the desire to search for my birth mother was fading from memory. At the closure of this incredible voyage, the need to find my biological roots and threads was not so pressing because, in many ways, I had found what I was searching for. For the first time, I was shaping my identity and becoming the woman I wanted to be, on my own terms. These became the women I leaned on as my own sister pulled away from me and fell deeply into addiction. And these were the women who held me up when my sister died. I came to accept that, like millions of adopted Americans, I would likely never reconnect with my birth family, my birth community. These ship mothers would become enough, and even more than enough, in that they charted a course of redefining what motherhood could be.

In her memoir *All You Can Ever Know*, Nicole Chung describes a very different birth mother journey, with a different ending. Chung began searching for her birth family while she was in her early twenties. When she was twenty-six years old and pregnant with her own daughter, she found them. By 1981, when Chung was born, more adoptions were open or semi-open, even when orchestrated through private agencies. And, although Chung's birth parents and adoptive parents all agreed to a closed adoption, Chung was able to connect with her birth family because of a Washington state law, passed in 2014, that allowed adoptees born before 1993 restricted access to their original birth records. Adoptees could pay a fee to work with a confidential intermediary to negotiate communication with birth parents, although birth parents could still request to withhold identifying information from adoptees.[1] This presented a small window but a window nonetheless for Chung, and she chose to jump through it.

Chung was born in Washington State to parents who had recently immigrated from Korea. She was adopted soon after birth by a white family in Oregon. Growing up in a small town as one of the few people of color, a child who clearly stood apart from her white parents, Chung would hear statements like "Where did they get you?" or "How much did you cost?"[2] The sting of being different, of standing out, was especially wounding for Chung as a transracial adoptee. As Chung describes her childhood growing up in a white town and a white family, "I had been convinced that my biggest flaw, my physical appearance, was offensive and irredeemable."[3] Her stark physical separateness from her adoptive family was part of Chung's catalyst for embarking on her own voyage to find her birth family. Like mine, Chung's adoption was orchestrated through an attorney and a private adoption agency. But our six-year age difference already significantly impacted how adoption transactions, even in the private sector, were negotiated. And less restrictive adoption search laws in Washington made the search possible.

When Chung was pregnant with her first child, she took the huge step of hiring an intermediary and negotiating opening contact with her birth family. Like me, her impending journey as a mother brought on complicated emotions that made denying the significance of her own adoption impossible. While Chung was in her third trimester of pregnancy, her adoption search intermediary connected her with her birth file. For the first time in her life, she learned that she had two sisters and that her first name, given by her birth parents, was Susan. "I felt as though I had been staring at a waiting chessboard all my life, and now the dusty old pieces were finally starting to move."[4] With the guidance of the intermediary, Chung sent off a letter to her birth mother and her birth father, requesting to connect.

Just weeks before the birth of her first child, Chung started communicating with her birth sisters. Through phone calls and emails, she would learn that both her sisters had been told that she had died at birth. Her birth parents were struggling financially when Chung was born, and the impending medical bills around her premature birth and health complications drove the decision to give her up for adoption. The lie that she died at birth covered up complications and shame her parents feared they might face from their community for giving birth to a sickly child. Chung also learned that her older sister was mercilessly beaten by her birth mother her entire childhood. Her birth father had advocated for Chung's adoption not just for financial reasons but also, perhaps, subconsciously understanding the future trauma that she could experience if she were raised by her abusive birth mother. On the day Chung went into labor, she received an email from her birth father. It opened with, "Dear Nicole, I received your letter. Please forgive me."[5]

Chung chose not to connect with her birth mother, but she would go on to forge a deep, lasting relationship with her older birth sister. Their own children, blood cousins, are growing up together. And Chung and her sister are learning together and leaning on each other as they become the mothers their own mother could not be for them.

Chung's adoption reunification story is full of complications, disappointments, and pain. It is also full of hope and love and demonstrates the power of truth-telling after decades of lies. In the opening of her memoir, Chung shares an experience she had at the very beginning of her own adoption search journey. When Chung had just graduated from college, a young couple hoping to adopt a child asked to meet with her to talk about her experience with adoption. They asked her if she ever felt that her adoptive parents weren't her real parents. They asked if there had ever been any issues around her adoption when she was growing up. And they asked if she had ever minded not being white like her adoptive parents. Each question was like a sucker punch because it nailed the duplicitous state of adoption in America. Each question alluded to the complexity of adoption and a fraught societal desire to ignore the difficulties and traumas around adoption.

This couple desperately held to a naive hope that they could somehow make their adoption simple, insignificant, and easy. In the conclusion of *American Baby*, Gabrielle Glaser writes:

Adoptive parents, who provide nurture and love with the very best of intentions, must also understand that adoption always equates to loss for the adoptee. People who are adopted are often told that they are "lucky." . . . But there is no dispute that their families love them, and in that sense, of course, they are lucky. But love and devotion can only go so far in annulling loss, even if—especially if—it is not verbalized. So often in adoption, each party carries grief.[6]

This adopting couple wanted to ensure that grief and loss were not part of their potential adoption experience. And as Chung struggled to answer this earnest young couple, she felt "something like panic, the sudden shame of being found out."[7] What she didn't want to share then but poignantly shares in her memoir is that adoption *always* includes loss.

The questions that the couple failed to ask were about Chung's experiences navigating her identity and the reasons for her adoption, questions about the ties that would be severed through the adoption process, and the impact that would have on how Chung saw herself in a family that didn't look like her. How did Chung's birth parents feel about giving her up? Was that choice given freely? Was it made under duress and in a state of chaos? Did her birth family have support, or were they in need of support when she was given up? Those were the questions everyone needed to ask leading up to an adoption. Even if a baby grows up in a loving, nurturing family like Chung's, if these questions aren't asked, the trauma continues. And that trauma lands on all members of the adopting triad.

Nicole Chung chose to stay deeply connected with her adoptive parents and conscientiously not to form a bond with her birth mother. But she was able to make this choice independently and with agency only once she knew the truth about her birth and adoption and fully understood the circumstances of her birth family. It is the truth about her own history, and the autonomy to navigate her familial connections moving forward, that set Chung free. I have made peace with the likelihood that I will never know the truth about my conception, my birth, or the circumstances around my adoption. I will never know my birth family or learn what my birth mother went through while she was pregnant with me and relinquished me. To fill this space of unknowing, I have sewn new threads of nonbiological family connections with my ship mothers, friends, and in-laws. And I am weaving new biological threads with my daughters as I watch them grow and become their own women. These connections have created strong and lasting bonds that give me new roots that tether me to the top of my identity triangle.

The nature versus nurture debate does not have a clear winner and loser. What does win in the end is choice and truth. Adoption can operate with integrity and in the best interest of all members of the adopting triad. But this can happen only when it is done with full transparency and through choice and free will on the parts of the relinquishing mother, the adoptive parents, and the child. Policy and practice should center family preservation when possible and follow UNICEF's guidelines in the Convention on the Rights of the Child, which state that adoption should always be a last resort for a child and that "families needing support to care for their children should receive it, and that alternative means of caring for a child should only be considered when, despite this assistance, a child's family is unavailable, unable or unwilling to care for her or him."[8] If adoption as a last resort is necessary, it is vital that adoptees know their biological pasts and that the adoptions are conducted in open processes. When adoptions are closed and children are completely severed from their biological pasts, they are also severed from knowing, processing, and understanding the nature side of their identities. We are all a combination of both nature and nurture, and it is our human right to understand how both have influenced our identities. Again, what wins in the end is choice and truth.

Ethical adoption also requires women to have autonomy over their bodies and their choices around their fertility. It necessitates women being valued and supported in those choices by their broader community, whether that means choosing to terminate a pregnancy or carrying a baby to term to keep it or relinquish it for adoption. But this is not how most adoptions in the United States operated historically. The history of adoption in America is defined by deceit, lies, and policies that weaponize "bad" women's fertility as a commodity to be used against them. Our society continues to dehumanize mothers deemed bad, particularly poor mothers and mothers of color, which then justifies policies and practices that strip women of their fertility autonomy and parental autonomy. As long as adoption practices depend on the dehumanization of people involved in the adoption transaction, it will continue to traumatize our nation.

Both domestic and transnational adoptions have plummeted in the past two decades. In the United States, we have seen a particularly precipitous decline in transnational adoptions.[9] Research and activism, particularly in transnational adoption, have uncovered the rampant human rights abuses steeped in misogynistic ideas of who is worthy of mothering and who is unworthy of mothering. Growing public awareness of these abuses, coupled with geopolitical shifts that have curbed transnational adoption transactions, are beginning to change how Americans view the commodification of international babies and children, a market that for decades was defined by altruism. Domestic adoptions in the United States have been on a consistent decline since their peak in the early 1970s, prior to the passage of the 1973 *Roe v. Wade* ruling. As women gained autonomy over their bodies, many of the circumstances that facilitated a booming adoption market—forced pregnancies, lack of prenatal care and community support, and personal financial and social crises connected to unplanned pregnancy—were mitigated. And the domestic adoption market lost its supply chain. Adoption practices and fertility autonomy are inextricably linked.

The 2022 *Dobbs v. Jackson Women's Health Organization* ruling, federally overturning women's reproductive rights, is a harbinger of a return to this weaponization of fertility and the dehumanization of women as we look ahead to an upward surge in adoption in the post-*Roe* era. In the *Dobbs* decision, Justices Barrett and Alito referenced this decline in adoptable babies. During argumentation in the *Dobbs* hearing, Barret cited "safe haven" laws, laws that protect parents who want to relinquish unwanted infants at hospitals. In her questioning, Barrett asked, "Insofar as you and many of your *amici* [supporting legal briefs] focus on the ways in which the forced parenting, forced motherhood would hinder women's access to the workplace and to equal opportunities, it's also focused on the consequences of parenting and the obligations of motherhood that flow from pregnancy. Why don't the safe haven laws take care of that problem?"[10] In Barrett's logic, the act of leaving a newborn at the hospital after birth fully relieves a birth mother and birth community of all the obligations of motherhood and parenting, or, as she characterizes it, "the problem." Barrett, in her ruling, is requiring the nation to reengage with a fantasy that adoption is simple and easy and is a pacifying solution to an unplanned pregnancy.

In Barrett's vision, the act of forcing a woman to carry a baby to term, without options, without bodily autonomy, is an unproblematic quick fix to the consequences and obligations of parenting. The history of adoption in America proves the fallacy of her thinking. But Barrett, as a white, Christian, privileged adopting mother of two transracial children, has a personal investment in believing in this fantasy. For millions of Americans, Justice Barrett embodies the archetype of the savior-like adoptive mother—like Bertha Holt, who could pluck babies out of despair, chaos, and "savagery" and raise them in a valued, model American family.

The *Dobbs* ruling directly represents the intricate connection between adoption and fertility. In his opinion, Justice Alito directly tied the shrinking supply of adoptable babies to the justifications for abolishing reproductive rights for women when he wrote,

> Americans who believe that abortion should be restricted press countervailing arguments about modern developments. They note that attitudes about the pregnancy of unmarried women have changed drastically; that federal and state laws ban discrimination on the basis of pregnancy; that leave for pregnancy and childbirth are now guaranteed by law in many cases; that the costs of medical care associated with pregnancy are covered by insurance or government assistance; that States have increasingly adopted "safe haven" laws, which generally allow women to drop off babies anonymously; and that a woman who puts her newborn up for adoption today has little reason to fear that the baby will not find a suitable home.[11]

Like Barrett, Alito was attempting to paint an easy, unproblematic picture of pregnancy in America, claiming that pregnant women are not discriminated against in the workplace, that women have access to affordable prenatal care, and that—similar to Barrett's claim—it is easy and simple to relinquish a newborn through safe haven laws.

Again, our nation's history with adoption and family social welfare directly contradicts the picture Alito paints. Millions of pregnant women, particularly those of color and those locked in cycles of poverty, experience none of these "modern developments.'" Currently, the states that have banned abortions also have the highest rates of uninsured women and the weakest maternal support for pregnant women.[12] Requiring women to endure forced pregnancies with a false promise that they will be cared for and that relinquishing their babies will be simple and easy, that they can walk away from the experience unscathed, is preposterous and damaging.

But what this fallacious promise is sure to do is ensure a resupply of adoptable babies. In the final footnote to his above-quoted opinion, Alito cites the fact that as of 2002 nearly one million American women were seeking to adopt children but that "the domestic supply of infants relinquished at birth or within the first month of life and available to be adopted had become virtually nonexistent."[13]

The virtually nonexistent supply of infants relinquished at birth coincides unsurprisingly with consistently abated fertility rates in the United States. Between 1958 and 1978, fertility rates in the United States plummeted from an average of 3.5 children per woman to 1.7. From then, the rate incrementally climbed up to 2.05 in 2008. But over the past fifteen years, the rate again decreased and then flatlined by 2020 at a rate of 1.7, the same rate as in 1978.[14] The majority decision in the *Dobbs* ruling, which imposes forced pregnancies on millions of American women, can be seen as a direct response to the decline in fertility rates, coupled with an increased demand for adoptable babies. Again, adoption markets are intricately linked to fertility.

The philosophy that has permeated adoption policy over the past hundred years, which emphasizes the needs and rights of adoptive families over the needs and rights of the birth mother and her community, is being reignited in this post-*Roe* era. The focus is on the fetus, at the expense of the birth mother and her community and even of the life of that child *after* it is born. According to the majority opinion in the *Dobbs* ruling, forcing women to carry babies to term and then give them up for adoption is not a problem. In fact, for both Barrett and Alito, it is a viable solution to the demands of the adoption market.

The day after the Supreme Court overturned *Roe v. Wade*, legal scholar and civil rights advocate Kimberlé Crenshaw issued a response, in collaboration with the African American Policy Forum, titled "Our Statement on Bodily Autonomy." In it, she wrote, "The consequences of our society's failure to see coerced pregnancy as a legacy of enslavement have descended once again upon Black women and all pregnant people with lethal force. Had the project of liberation from enslavement been rooted in this recognition, then coerced childbirth would have been prohibited as a foundational principle of freedom."[15] Crenshaw was referring to our nation's history of chattel slavery, in which it was not only acceptable but also profitable for white enslavers to rape enslaved women and then sell their children into slavery.[16] Her scathing critique of *Dobbs* provides a powerful link between fertility rights, family structures, and mothers' variegated value in American culture. Already in the post-*Roe* world, we are seeing that it is largely poor women who are carrying the burden of forced pregnancies.[17] Wealthy women continue to have access to prenatal care, reproductive health care, and, most important, choice. As it was one hundred years ago, women in poverty today are becoming targets of market forces that commodify their fertility. And as it was one hundred years ago, the savior in this new post-*Roe* story will be the hegemonic adoptive mother. Our nation is saved from the destitution of the impoverished "bad" mother by the grace and altruism of the "good" mother, and the baby is transferred between them.

The good and the bad mother exist and are perpetuated by their codependence as binaries. This means that the ideal of the good mother can exist only when we also subscribe to the equally negative image of the bad mother. The good mother, who epitomizes hegemonic mothering, is everything that a bad mother is not. What the hegemonic mother is not is single, on welfare, an immigrant, or a woman of color. This binary is perpetuated as long as we subscribe to a hegemonic image of the ideal good mother and demonize any woman who lands outside its confines. When a woman does not have the respect and free choice to terminate a pregnancy or to keep or relinquish her baby, and is forced to carry a baby to term in order to give it up, adoption operates as a conduit between these two opposites, moving that baby away from the bad and toward the good. Women have existed and do exist in this impossible paradox of societal shame surrounding both fertility and infertility, and adoption sits at the crossroads. So much of relieving the trauma of adoption involves transforming our perceptions of motherhood and blowing this binary apart.

Nefertiti Austin powerfully summarizes the toxic binary of good versus bad mother when she explains,

> I was already an outlier in the Black community for adopting a child I did not know and was not related to. I was an outlier in the white community for adopting a child domestically and the butt of jokes by male coworkers who didn't believe I could raise a boy on my own. As a writer, I was fighting against white privilege's erasure of Black parenting perspectives and insistence that the mother automatically meant white. The denial of voices of color meant our children's lives did not matter. Motherhood was supposed to be fun, filled with challenges to bring the best out of our kids and ourselves. For me, and for all Black mothers in America, it was alternatively fun and harrowing, as we broached conversations no parent should ever have to have with their young children.[18]

Austin is calling us to create a world where a Black adoptive single mother can be celebrated and valued. History has repeatedly relegated mothers of color and single mothers to a corner of shame, forcibly taken away their babies, and sterilized them. It is now more important than ever to stop this erasure of Black mothering and all mothering experiences that have been silenced, delegitimized, and even criminalized for not being good enough.

Blowing apart the restrictive binary of mothering requires all of us to redefine what mothering is and who has access to it. The

Merriam-Webster Dictionary variously defines the verb form of "mother" as to give rise to, to care for and protect.[19] This is an all-inclusive action of love that anybody can practice: men, women, nonbinary-identifying people, people of color, people who have children, and people who do not have children. In her book *The Truth Will Set You Free, but First It Will Piss You Off!* Gloria Steinem taps directly into this transformative and inclusive idea of understanding mothering as a verb. She writes,

> Even if we are not mothers, the noun, we may be mothering, the verb. Indeed, unless mothering is a verb, it is not an action in the world. Think about it: As a noun, mother is limited to half the human race, and also to the accident of fertility and age and intention. In some societies motherhood is honored only in women who are married or who have sons. In most societies, a woman is encouraged to give birth to another person more than she is encouraged to give birth to herself. As a noun, mother may be good or bad, willing or unwilling, on welfare or rich, worshipped or blamed, dominating or nurturing, accidental or chosen. . . . But when mother is a verb—as in to be mothered and to mother—ah, then the very best of human possibilities come into our imaginations. To mother is to care about the welfare of another person so much as one's own. To mother depends on empathy and thoughtfulness, noticing and caring.[20]

Can a woman be a mother even if she has never given birth to or raised a child? Can a single mother of color be revered as a mother? Can two men mother? Can a nonbinary person give birth to and mother a child? My answer to all of these is yes. When we expand our perspective of who can mother, we step out of the destructive good-bad mother binary that has perpetuated abusive adoption practices for decades.

My ship mothers taught me to see how an expansive view of mothering can impact a community. As lighthouses and truth-tellers, they also helped me to redefine myself as a woman and a mother. As adoptions increase in the post-*Roe* era, as they inevitably will, it is especially important that we don't fall back into the pattern of commodifying babies through adoption transactions at the expense of birth mothers whom our society deems unqualified and devalued. This is especially important at this precarious time when millions of women are losing autonomy over their reproductive rights, their bodies, and their ability to mother, or *not* mother, on their own terms. When Sandy White Hawk, founder of the First Nations Repatriation Institute and survivor of the IAP, counsels potential adopting parents, she presents them with the stark reality of adoption: "We are a commodity as adopted kids. We really are. Somebody will make money off of your child that you will receive. So you need to be extra scrutinizing that you will not be told lies."[21] Knowing where that child came from, the circumstances of the child's birth, and the experience of the birth mother and birth community is vital to engaging in adoption that promotes healing instead of trauma.

My journey began with my deep need to find a sea anchor, a form of stability in the storm, to guide me through rough waters. My sea anchor now takes form in the amazing women, the lighthouses I lean on to guide me in my journey as a woman and mother. My sea anchor is also the family I have created, whose biological and nonbiological bonds keep me upright when seas are rough. My sister didn't have those lighthouses in her life, and in the end, she couldn't find her bearings and went down. I hope that in writing these stories, I can throw out a lifeline of connection to my sister, wherever she may be, and she can know that there is a sea anchor for her too.

Notes

Introduction

1. Lithwick, "Horrifying Implications of Alito's Most Alarming Footnote."
2. Carp, *Adoption in America*, 1.
3. "Parenting in America: 1. The American Family Today," Pew Research Center, December 17, 2015, https://www.pewresearch.org/social-trends/2015/12/17/1-the-american-family-today/.
4. "Topics in Adoption History: Adoption Statistics."

Chapter 1. Adoption

1. "Milestones for Women in American Politics."
2. Vance, *Adoption History*, 18.
3. US Census Bureau, "Living Arrangements of Children: 1960 to Present."
4. Wegar, "Adoption, Family Ideology, and Social Stigma," 363.
5. Wegar, 364.
6. Wegar, 365.
7. Wegar, 366.
8. Carp, *Adoption in America*, 2.
9. Herman, *Kinship by Design*, 22.
10. Herman, 47.
11. Herman, 28.
12. Herman, 25.
13. Carp, *Family Matters*, 9.
14. Carp, 10.
15. Vance, *Adoption History*, 52.
16. Herman, *Kinship by Design*, 13.
17. Adams, *Education for Extinction*, 54.
18. Adams, 54.
19. Carp, *Family Matters*, 9.

20. Herman, *Kinship by Design*, 57.
21. Herman, 43.
22. Carp, *Adoption Politics*, 7–11.
23. Carp, 7–8.
24. Carp, 10.
25. Carp, 11.
26. Carp, *Adoption in America*, 219.
27. Carp, *Adoption in America*, 193.
28. Carp, *Adoption Politics*, 7–11.
29. Carp, *Adoption in America*, 211.
30. Wegar, *Adoption, Identity, and Kinship*, 58; US Department of Health and Human Services, "How Common Is Infertility?"
31. Carp, *Adoption in America*, 208.
32. Carp, *Adoption in America*, 210.
33. Carp, *Adoption Politics*, 12.
34. Carp, *Adoption Politics*, 12.
35. Wegar, *Adoption, Identity, and Kinship*, 54.
36. Wegar, 53.
37. Carp, *Adoption in America*, 16.
38. Carp, *Adoption in America*, 16.
39. Wilson-Buterbaugh, *Baby Scoop Era*, 60.
40. Wilson-Buterbaugh, 67.
41. Wilson-Buterbaugh, 73–74.
42. Wegar, *Adoption, Identity, and Kinship*, 54.

Chapter 2. Assimilation

1. Roszia and Maxon, *Seven Core Issues*, 68–69.
2. Myong and Bissenbakker, "Attachment as Affective Assimilation," 174.
3. Myong and Bissenbakker, 166.
4. Harness, *Bitterroot*, 9.
5. Lomawaima, *They Called It Prairie Light*, 6.
6. Lomawaima, 30.
7. Bertolt, "After the Meriam Report," 3.
8. Jacobs, *Generation Removed*, 13.
9. Jacobs, 7.
10. Thibeault and Spencer, "Indian Adoption Project," 807.
11. Thibeault and Spencer, 807.
12. Jacobs, *Generation Removed*, 53.
13. Jacobs, 12.
14. Thibeault and Spencer, "Indian Adoption Project," 809.
15. Jacobs, *Generation Removed*, 17.
16. Thibeault and Spencer, "Indian Adoption Project," 812.
17. Thibeault and Spencer, 814.
18. Jacobs, *Generation Removed*, 20.

19. Thibeault and Spencer, "Indian Adoption Project," 815.

20. Jacobs, *Generation Removed*, 31.

21. Jacobs, 127.

22. Jacobs, 101.

23. Thibeault and Spencer, "Indian Adoption Project," 815.

24. Harness, *Mixing Cultural Identities*, 57.

25. Lawrence, "Indian Health Service and the Sterilization of Native American Women," 400.

26. Shepherd, "Enemy is the Knife," 90.

27. Jacobs, *Generation Removed*, 7.

28. Jacobs, 26. From Brownlee's article "The American Indian Child," published in the journal *Children* in 1958.

29. Anderson, *Recognition of Being*, 158.

30. Jacobs, *Generation Removed*, 39.

31. Thibeault and Spencer, "Indian Adoption Project," 809.

32. Lawrence, "Indian Health Service and the Sterilization of Native American Women," 412.

33. Shepherd, "Enemy is the Knife," 95.

34. Lawrence, "Indian Health Service and the Sterilization of Native American Women," 402.

35. Lawrence, 412.

36. Lawrence, 412.

37. Lawrence, 412.

38. Lawrence, 410.

39. Thibeault and Spencer, "Indian Adoption Project," 810.

40. Jacobs, *Generation Removed*, 151.

41. Harness, *Bitterroot*, 10.

42. "About Me," Susan Devan Harness Author of *Bitterroot: A Salish Memoir of Transracial Adoption* (website), https://susanharness.com/about/.

43. Harness, *Bitterroot*, 47.

44. Susan Harness, interview with author, September 14, 2022.

45. Harness, *Bitterroot*, 22.

46. Hentz, *Two Worlds*, 38.

47. Harness, *Mixing Cultural Identities*, 123.

48. Harness, *Mixing Cultural Identities*, 125.

49. Harness, *Bitterroot*, 324.

50. Kuwahara, *Tattoo*, 33–39.

51. Kuwahara, 2.

Chapter 3. Birth

1. Roszia and Maxon, *Seven Core Issues*, 19.

2. Roszia and Maxon, 21.

3. *Dead Men on Furlough*.

4. Winslow, "Immigration Law," 319–49.

5. Joanne Lee, "The Holt Adoption Agency: Changing the Face of America's Social and Ethnic Relations," Dartmouth University, accessed July 19, 2023, www.dartmouth.edu/~hist32/History/S29%20-%20Holt%20Agency.htm.

6. Winslow, "Immigration Law," 321.

7. Winslow, 320.

8. Vance, *Adoption History*, 116.

9. Vance, 119.

10. Winslow, "Immigration Law," 319–49.

11. Winslow, 322.

12. Vance, *Adoption History*, 113.

13. Vance, 114.

14. Vance, 111.

15. "Who We Are: Our History," American Mothers, accessed July 19, 2023, www.americanmothers.org/who-we-are/our-history/.

16. "Who We Are: Our History."

17. "People and Organizations: Bertha and Harry Holt."

18. "People and Organizations: Bertha and Harry Holt."

19. Holt International (website), www.holtinternational.org.

20. Sachs, *Life We Were Given*, 3.

21. Sachs, 7, 8.

22. Taylor quoted in Sachs, 36.

23. Sachs, *Life We Were Given*, 33.

24. Sachs, 13.

25. Sachs, 13.

26. Sachs, 3–16.

27. Weaver, *Ideologies of Forgetting*, 1.

28. Weaver, 7.

29. Sachs, *Life We Were Given*, 53.

30. Sachs, 55.

31. *Time* article quoted in Sachs, xiii.

32. Gesteira et al., "Child Appropriations and Irregular Adoptions," 586.

33. Chambers, "Chile's Stolen Children."

34. Gesteira et al., "Child Appropriations and Irregular Adoptions," 590.

35. Lefferman et al., "American Firefighter Learns He's One of Chile's Stolen Children."

36. Lefferman et al.

37. Jacobson, *Culture Keeping*, 5.

38. "International Adoption Rate in U.S. Doubled in the 1990s."

39. Laronal quoted in Weaver, *Routledge International Handbook of Indigenous Resilience*, 240.

Chapter 4. Motherhood

1. Tichenor et al., "Variation in Attitudes toward Being a Mother," 601.

2. Tichenor et al., 602.

3. Laskin, "How Parental Liability Statutes Criminalize and Stigmatize Minority Mothers," 2.
4. Laskin, 4.
5. Laskin, 8.
6. Austin, *Motherhood So White*, 120.
7. Austin, 29.
8. National Association of Black Social Workers, "Position Statement on Trans-racial Adoptions."
9. Briggs, *Taking Children*, 19–20.
10. Austin, *Motherhood So White*, 66.
11. Austin, 69.
12. Austin, 66.
13. Begos et al., *Against Their Will*, iii, 2.
14. Begos et al., v.
15. Carp, *Adoption in America*, 232.
16. Kaelber, "Eugenics: Compulsory Sterilization in 50 American States."
17. Begos et al., *Against Their Will*, 6.
18. Begos et al., iii.
19. Begos et al., 5.
20. Bruinius, *Better for All the World*, 6.
21. Begos et al., *Against Their Will*, 2, 9.
22. Bruinius, *Better for All the World*, 5.
23. Begos et al., *Against Their Will*, 9.
24. Feldstein, *Motherhood in Black and White*, 13.
25. Feldstein, 12.
26. Carp, *Adoption in America*, 13.
27. Feldstein, *Motherhood in Black and White*, 1.
28. Jacobs, *Generation Removed*, 69.
29. Jacobs, 70.
30. Feldstein, *Motherhood in Black and White*, 47.
31. Jacobs, *Generation Removed*, 53.
32. Jacobs, xxxiii.
33. Ackerman, *Necessary Balance*, 54.
34. Sarah Newcomb, phone interview and email correspondence with author, 2021.
35. Patel, "Forced Sterilization of Women as Discrimination."
36. Alvarez, "Whistleblower Alleges High Rate of Hysterectomies and Medical Neglect."
37. Fessler, *Girls Who Went Away*, 104.
38. Fessler, 108.
39. Fessler, 29, 30, 134.
40. Fessler, 137, 107, 108.
41. Fessler, 138, 142.
42. Ellerby, *Embroidering the Scarlet A*, 5.
43. Fessler, *Girls Who Went Away*, 19.

Chapter 5. Death

1. Glaser, *American Baby*, 138.
2. Carp, *Family Matters*, 15.
3. Ward, *White Welfare State*, 1.
4. Ward, 29.
5. Ward, 30.
6. Ward, 1.
7. Floyd et al., "TANF Policies Reflect Racist Legacy of Cash Assistance."
8. Floyd et al.
9. Floyd et al.
10. Ward, *White Welfare State*, 9.
11. Wilson-Buterbaugh, *Baby Scoop Era*, 55.
12. Wilson-Buterbaugh, 48.
13. Wilson-Buterbaugh, 39.
14. William R. Johnston, comp., "Historical Statistics on Adoption in the United States, Plus Statistics on Child Population and Welfare," Johnston's Archive (website), updated November 12, 2022, www.johnstonsarchive.net /policy/adoptionstats.html.
15. Wilson-Buterbaugh, *Baby Scoop Era*, 59.
16. Wilson-Buterbaugh, 67.
17. Glaser, *American Baby*, 67.
18. Glaser, 68.
19. Glaser, 74.
20. Glaser, 83.
21. Glaser, 85.
22. Glaser, 90.
23. National Association of Social Workers, "Code of Ethics," October 13, 1960, www.socialworkers.org/About/Ethics/Code-of-Ethics/g/LinkClick.aspx ?fileticket=lPpjxmAsCTs%3d&portalid=0.
24. Glaser, *American Baby*, 139–40.
25. Briggs, *Taking Children*, 108–10.
26. *Philadelphia Inquirer* quoted in Floyd et al., "TANF Policies Reflect Racist Legacy of Cash Assistance."
27. Floyd et al.
28. Floyd et al.
29. Floyd et al.
30. Floyd et al.
31. Briggs, *Taking Children*, 122.
32. US Department of Health and Human Services, "Recent Demographic Trends in Foster Care."
33. Briggs, *Taking Children*, 124.
34. Dickerson, "'We Need to Take Children Away,'" 42.
35. Briggs, *Taking Children*, 145.
36. Dickerson, "'We Need to Take Children Away,'" 66.
37. Thompson, "Court Rules for Deportee on Custody."

38. Dickerson, "'We Need to Take Children Away,'" 76.

39. Dickerson, 74.

40. Thibeault and Spencer, "Indian Adoption Project and the Profession of Social Work," 829.

41. Attorney-General's Department, "National Apology for Forced Adoptions," Australian Government, March 26, 2013, https://www.ag.gov.au/families -and-marriage/national-apology-forced-adoptions.

42. "International Campaigns," Movement for an Adoption Apology, accessed July 19, 2023, movementforanadoptionapology.org/links/.

Chapter 6. Reclaiming

1. Maxtone-Graham quoted in Melosh, *Strangers and Kin*, 246.

2. Melosh, 241.

3. "About," Alma Society (website), thealmasociety.org/about/.

4. Melosh, *Strangers and Kin*, 243.

5. "Document Archives: Jean M. Paton, *The Adopted Break Silence*, 1954."

6. Carp, *Jean Paton and the Struggle to Reform American Adoption*.

7. "Document Archives: Jean M. Paton, *The Adopted Break Silence*, 1954."

8. Carp, *Jean Paton and the Struggle to Reform American Adoption*, 10.

9. "People and Organizations: Bastard Nation."

10. Sotiropoulos, "Open Adoption and the Politics of Transnational Feminist Human Rights," 179–90.

11. "Convention on the Rights of the Child," UNICEF, accessed July 19, 2023, unicef.org/child-rights-convention.

12. Fogg-Davis, *Ethics of Transracial Adoption*.

13. Carp, *Jean Paton and the Struggle to Reform American Adoption*, 19.

14. Bell, *Black Power Movement and American Social Work*, 136.

15. Bell, 137.

16. National Association of Black Social Workers, "Position Statement on Trans-Racial Adoptions."

17. "Intercountry Adoption," UNICEF, June 26, 2015, www.unicef.org /media/intercountry-adoption.

18. Bell, *Black Power Movement and American Social Work*, 137.

19. "First-Time National Exposure for Mothers of Adoption Loss: CUB Founder, Lee Campbell, Speaks Out," Concerned United Birthparents, YouTube (47:38), posted July 14, 2014, www.youtube.com/watch?v=qz8LV2_DsSM.

20. Melosh, *Strangers and Kin*, 255.

21. "First-Time National Exposure for Mothers of Adoption Loss."

22. Jenni Bergal, "With Push from Adoptees, States Open Access to Birth Records," *Stateline* (blog), August 12, 2016, Pew Charitable Trusts, www .pewtrusts.org/en/research-and-analysis/blogs/stateline/2016/08/12/with-push -from-adoptees-states-open-access-to-birth-records.

23. "Where and How to Get an Original Pre-adoption Birth Certificate (If You Can Get One at All)," United States of OBC, accessed July 19, 2023,

adopteerightslaw.com/united-states-obc/. Those eleven states include Alabama, Alaska, Colorado, Connecticut, Kansas, Louisiana, Maine, New Hampshire, New York, Oregon, and Rhode Island.

24. Bergal, "With Push from Adoptees, States Open Access to Birth Records."

25. Bergal.

26. Pennsylvania Catholic Conference, "Testimony on House Bill 1262," April 14, 2015, www.legis.state.pa.us/WU01/LI/TR/Transcripts/2015_0056 _0009_TSTMNY.pdf.

27. Bergal, "With Push from Adoptees, States Open Access to Birth Records."

28. "About the Fair," Rosebud Sioux Tribe's Wacipi, Fair & Rodeo, accessed July 19, 2023, www.rosebudfair.com/about.

29. Sandy White Hawk, phone conversation with author, September 26, 2022.

30. White Hawk phone conversation.

31. *Blood Memory*.

32. *Blood Memory*.

33. White Hawk, *Child of the Indian Race*, 96.

34. Sandy White Hawk, phone conversation with author, September 26, 2022.

35. "Indian Child Welfare Act of 1978," Tribal Law and Policy Institute, Tribal Court Clearinghouse, www.tribal-institute.org/lists/chapter21_icwa.htm.

36. *Blood Memory*.

37. Landers et al., "American Indian and White Adoptees," 69.

38. Sandy White Hawk, phone conversation with author, September 14, 2022.

39. *Blood Memory*.

40. Sandy White Hawk, phone conversation with author, September 14, 2022.

41. *Blood Memory*.

42. Abby Budiman and Mark Hugo Lopez, "Amid Decline in International Adoptions to U.S., Boys Outnumber Girls for the First Time," Pew Research Center, October 17, 2017, www.pewresearch.org/fact-tank/2017/10/17/amid -decline-in-international-adoptions-to-u-s-boys-outnumber-girls-for-the-first -time/.

43. Sotiropoulos, "Open Adoption and the Politics of Transnational Feminist Human Rights," 186.

44. Bartholet et al., "Celebrity Adoptions and the Real World."

45. www.holtinternational.org/myth-i-cant-afford-adoption/.

46. Smolin, "Child Laundering," 116.

47. Baden, "Intercountry Adoption."

48. "An Adoption Gone Wrong," *Morning Edition*, National Public Radio, July 24, 2007, www.npr.org/2007/07/24/12185524/an-adoption-gone-wrong.

49. *Blood Memory*.

Chapter 7. Rebirth

1. "Where and How to Get an Original Pre-adoption Birth Certificate (If You Can Get One at All)," United States of OBC (website), accessed July 19, 2023, adopteerightslaw.com/united-states-obc/.

2. Chung, *All You Can Ever Know*, 9.

3. Chung, 53.

4. Chung, 111.

5. Chung, 111.

6. Glaser, *American Baby*, 274.

7. Chung, *All You Can Ever Know*, 6.

8. UNICEF, "Intercountry Adoption," June 26, 2015, www.unicef.org /media/intercountry-adoption.

9. Fenton, *End of International Adoption?*, 3.

10. Branigin, "Why Amy Coney Barrett's Questions about Adoption Worry Abortion Rights Activists."

11. Dobbs, State Health Officer of the Mississippi Department of Health, et al. v. Jackson Women's Health Organization et al., 33–34.

12. Treisman, "States with the Toughest Abortion Laws Have the Weakest Maternal Supports."

13. Dobbs v. Jackson, 34n46.

14. "U.S. Fertility Rate 1950–2023," Macrotrends, accessed July 19, 2023, www.macrotrends.net/countries/USA/united-states/fertility-rate.

15. African American Policy Forum, "Our Statement on Bodily Autonomy."

16. Briggs, *Taking Children*, 20.

17. Ryan, "'An Inequality Story.'"

18. Austin, *Motherhood So White*, 9.

19. *Merriam-Webster*, s.v. "mother," www.merriam-webster.com/dictionary /mother.

20. Steinem, *Truth Will Set You Free*, 17.

21. *Blood Memory*.

Bibliography

Books and Dissertations

Ackerman, Lillian A. *A Necessary Balance: Gender and Power among Indians of the Columbia Plateau.* Norman: University of Oklahoma Press, 2003.

Adams, David W. *Education for Extinction: American Indians and the Boarding School Experience, 1875–1928.* Lawrence: University Press of Kansas, 1995.

Anderson, Kim. *A Recognition of Being: Reconstructing Native Womanhood.* Toronto: Second Story Press, 2000.

Austin, Nefertiti. *Motherhood So White: A Memoir of Race, Gender, and Parenting in America.* Naperville, IL: Sourcebooks, 2019.

Balcom, Karen A. *The Traffic in Babies: Cross-Border Adoption and Baby-Selling between the United States and Canada, 1930–1972.* Toronto: University of Toronto Press, 2011.

Begos, Kevin P., Danielle Deaver, John Railey, and Scott Sexton. *Against Their Will: North Carolina's Sterilization Program.* Apalachicola, FL: Gray Oak Books, 2002.

Bell, Joyce M. *The Black Power Movement and American Social Work.* New York: Columbia University Press, 2014.

Bertolt, Jennifer L. "After the Meriam Report: W. Carson Ryan, Jr., and The Transformation of American Indian Education, 1928–1936." PhD diss., George Washington University, 2007.

Briggs, Laura. *Somebody's Children: The Politics of Transracial and Transnational Adoption.* Durham, NC: Duke University Press, 2012.

———. *Taking Children: A History of American Terror.* Oakland: University of California Press, 2020.

Bruinius, Harry. *Better for All the World: The Secret History of Forced Sterilization and America's Quest for Racial Purity.* New York: Random House, 2007.

Carp, E. W., ed. *Adoption in America: Historical Perspectives.* Ann Arbor: University of Michigan Press, 2002.

———. *Adoption Politics: Bastard Nation and Ballot Initiative 58.* Lawrence: University Press of Kansas, 2004.

————. *Family Matters: Secrecy and Disclosure in the History of Adoption.* Cambridge, MA: Harvard University Press, 1998.

————. *Jean Paton and the Struggle to Reform American Adoption.* Ann Arbor: University of Michigan Press, 2014.

Chung, Nicole. *All You Can Ever Know.* New York: Catapult, 2018.

Ellerby, Janet M. *Embroidering the Scarlet A: Unwed Mothers and Illegitimate Children in American Fiction and Film.* Ann Arbor: University of Michigan Press, 2015.

Fanshel, David. *Far from the Reservation: The Transracial Adoption of American Indian Children.* Metuchen, NJ: Scarecrow Press, 1972.

Farnham, Marynia, and Ferdinand Lundberg. *Modern Woman: The Lost Sex.* New York: Harper and Brothers, 1947.

Feldstein, Ruth. *Motherhood in Black and White: Race and Sex in American Liberalism, 1930–1965.* Ithaca, NY: Cornell University Press, 2000.

Fenton, Estye. *The End of International Adoption? An Unraveling Reproductive Market and the Politics of Healthy Babies.* New Brunswick, NJ: Rutgers University Press, 2019.

Fessler, Ann. *The Girls Who Went Away: The Hidden History of Women Who Surrendered Children for Adoption in the Decades before Roe v. Wade.* London: Penguin, 2006.

Fogg-Davis, Heath. *The Ethics of Transracial Adoption.* Ithaca, NY: Cornell University Press, 2002.

Glaser, Gabrielle. *American Baby: A Mother, a Child, and the Secret History of Adoption.* New York: Penguin Random House, 2021.

Harness, Susan D. *Bitterroot: A Salish Memoir of Transracial Adoption.* Lincoln: University of Nebraska Press, 2018.

————. *Mixing Cultural Identities through Transracial Adoption.* Lewiston, NY: Edwin Mellen Press, 2008.

Hentz, Trace L., ed. *Two Worlds: Lost Children of the Indian Adoption Projects.* Greenfield, MA: Blue Hand Books, 2017.

Herman, Ellen. *Kinship by Design: A History of Adoption in the Modern United States.* Chicago: University of Chicago Press, 2008.

Jacobs, Margaret D. *A Generation Removed: The Fostering and Adoption of Indigenous Children in the Postwar World.* Lincoln: University of Nebraska Press, 2014.

Jacobson, Heather. *Culture Keeping: White Mothers, International Adoption, and the Negotiation of Family Difference.* Nashville: Vanderbilt University Press, 2008.

Kim, Hosu. *Birth Mothers and Transnational Adoption Practice in South Korea: Virtual Mothering.* New York: Palgrave Macmillan, 2016.

Kluchin, Rebecca M. *Fit to Be Tied: Sterilization and Reproductive Rights in America, 1950–1980.* New Brunswick, NJ: Rutgers University Press, 2011.

Kuwahara, Makiko. *Tattoo: An Anthropology.* New York: Berg, 2005.

Lomawaima, K. T. *They Called It Prairie Light: The Story of Chilocco Indian School.* Lincoln: University of Nebraska Press, 1994.

Melosh, Barbara. *Strangers and Kin: The American Way of Adoption.* Cambridge, MA: Harvard University Press, 2002.

Mock, Janet. *Redefining Realness: My Path to Womanhood, Identity, Love and So Much More*. New York: Atria, 2014.

Payne, Mary S. *Adoption's Hidden History: From Native American Tribes to Locked Lives*. Vol. 1. N.p.: privately printed, 2013.

Roszia, Sharon, and Allison D. Maxon, eds. *Seven Core Issues in Adoption and Permanency: A Comprehensive Guide to Promoting Understanding and Healing in Adoption, Foster Care, Kinship Families and Third-Party Reproduction*. London: Jessica Kingsley, 2019.

Sachs, Dana. *The Life We Were Given: Operation Babylift, International Adoption, and the Children of War in Vietnam*. Boston: Beacon Press, 2010.

Shapiro, Dani. *Inheritance: A Memoir of Genealogy, Paternity, and Love*. New York: Penguin Random House, 2020.

Sorosky, Arthur D., Annette Baran, and Reuben Pannor. *The Adoption Triangle—Sealed or Opened Records: How They Affect Adoptees, Birth Parents, and Adoptive Parents*. New York: Doubleday, 1978.

Steinem, Gloria. *The Truth Will Set You Free, but First It Will Piss You Off!* New York: Random House, 2019.

Tuhiwai Smith, Linda, Eve Tuck, and K. Wayne Yang, eds. *Indigenous and Decolonizing Studies in Education*. New York: Routledge, 2019.

Vance, Janine (aka Janine Myung Ja). *Adoption History: An Adoptee's Research into Child Trafficking*. N.p.: privately printed, 2022.

Ward, Deborah E. *The White Welfare State: The Racialization of U.S. Welfare Policy*. Ann Arbor: University of Michigan Press, 2005.

Weaver, Gina M. *Ideologies of Forgetting: Rape in the Vietnam War*. Albany: State University of New York Press, 2010.

Weaver, Hilary N., ed. *The Routledge International Handbook of Indigenous Resilience*. New York: Routledge, 2022.

Wegar, Katarina. *Adoption, Identity, and Kinship: The Debate over Sealed Birth Records*. New Haven, CT: Yale University Press, 1997.

White Hawk, Sandy. *A Child of the Indian Race: A Story of Return*. St. Paul: Minnesota Historical Society Press, 2022.

Wilson-Buterbaugh, Karen. *The Baby Scoop Era: Unwed Mothers, Infant Adoption, Forced Surrender*. N.p.: privately printed, 2017.

Articles

Alvarez, Priscilla. "Whistleblower Alleges High Rate of Hysterectomies and Medical Neglect at ICE Facility." CNN. Last modified September 16, 2020. https://www.cnn.com/2020/09/15/politics/immigration-customs-enforcement-medical-care-detainees/index.html.

Amy, Jean-Jacques, and Sam Rowlands. "Legalised Non-consensual Sterilisation—Eugenics Put into Practice before 1945, and the Aftermath." Pt. 1, "USA, Japan, Canada, and Mexico." *European Journal of Contraception and Reproductive Health Care* 23, no. 2 (2018): 121–29. doi:10.1080/13625187.2018.1450973.

"Assembly of First Nations Pushes for Criminalization of Forced Sterilization of First Nations Women." Professional Services Close-Up: Gale OneFile Business. December 24, 2018. https://link.gale.com/apps/doc/A566970682 /GPS?u=wash_main&sid=GPS&xid=61ff2a0e.

Baccara, Mariagiovanna, Allan Collard-Wexler, Leonardo Felli, and Leeat Yariv. "Child-Adoption Matching: Preferences for Gender and Race." *American Economic Journal: Applied Economics* 6, no. 3 (2014): 133–58.

Baden, Amanda. "Intercountry Adoption: The Beginning of the End." Future of Adoption Series: Beyond Safety to Well-Being. Rudd Adoption Research Program at UMass Amherst, 2019.

Bartholet, Elizabeth, E. J. Graff, Marguerite A. Write, David Smolin, Diane B. Kunz, and Jane Aronson. "Celebrity Adoptions and the Real World." *New York Times*, May 10, 2009.

Blum, Ann S. "Adoption Politics: Families, Identities and Power." *Journal of Women's History* 27, no. 1 (2015): 168–77.

Branigin, Anne. "Why Amy Coney Barrett's Questions about Adoption Worry Abortion Rights Activists." *Lily.* Last modified December 1, 2021. https:// www.thelily.com/why-amy-coney-barretts-questions-about-adoption-worry -abortion-rights-activists/.

Broadhurst, Karen, and Claire Mason. "Birth Parents and the Collateral Consequences of Court-Ordered Child Removal: Towards a Comprehensive Framework." *International Journal of Law, Policy and the Family* 31, no. 1 (2017): 41–59.

Chambers, Jane. "Chile's Stolen Children: 'I Was Tricked into Handing Over My Baby.'" BBC News. Last modified September 26, 2019. https://www.bbc .com/news/world-latin-america-48929112.

Cooke, Kathy J. "Human Fertility and Differential Birth Rates in American Eugenics and Genetics." *Mount Sinai Journal of Medicine* 65, no. 3 (1998): 161–66.

Dickerson, Caitlin. "'We Need to Take Children Away': The Secret History of the U.S. Government's Family-Separation Policy." *Atlantic* 330, no. 2 (2022): 36–76.

Floyd, Ife, Ladonna Pavetti, Laura Meyer, Ali Safawi, Liz Schott, Evelyn Bellew, and Abigail Magnus. "TANF Policies Reflect Racist Legacy of Cash Assistance: Reimagined Program Should Center Black Mothers." Center on Budget and Policy Priorities, August 4, 2021. https://www.cbpp.org/research/family -income-support/tanf-policies-reflect-racist-legacy-of-cash-assistance.

Germain, Rosie. "Reading 'The Second Sex' in 1950s America." *Historical Journal* 56, no. 4 (2013): 1041–62.

Gesteira, Soledad, Irene Salvo Agoglia, Carla Villalta, and Karen Alfaro Monsalve. "Child Appropriations and Irregular Adoptions: Activism for the 'Right to Identity,' Justice, and Reparation in Argentina and Chile." *Childhood* 28, no. 4 (2021): 585–99.

Heikkila, Kim. "'Everybody Thinks It's Right to Give the Child Away': Unwed Mothers at Booth Memorial Hospital, 1961–63." *Minnesota History* 65, no. 6 (2017): 229–41.

Horsburgh, Beverly. "Schrodinger's Cat, Eugenics, and the Compulsory Sterilization of Welfare Mothers: Deconstructing an Old/New Rhetoric and Constructing the Reproductive Right to Natality for Low-Income Women of Color." *Cardozo Law Review* 17, no. 3 (1996): 531–82.

Landers, Ashley L., Sharon M. Danes, Kate Ingalls-Maloney, and Sandy White Hawk. "American Indian and White Adoptees: Are There Mental Health Differences?" *American Indian and Alaska Native Mental Health Research* 24, no. 2 (2017): 54–75.

Laskin, Elena. "How Parental Liability Statutes Criminalize and Stigmatize Minority Mothers." *American Criminal Law Review* 37, no. 3 (2000).

Lawrence, Jane. "The Indian Health Service and the Sterilization of Native American Women." *American Indian Quarterly* 24, no. 3 (2000): 400–419.

Lefferman, Jake, Zach Fannin, Jessica Hopper, and Haley Yamada. "American Firefighter Learns He's One of Chile's Stolen Children." ABC News. Last modified April 12, 2022. https://abcnews.go.com/Nightline/american-fire fighter-learns-chiles-stolen-children/story?id=84012146.

Lithwick, Dahlia. "The Horrifying Implications of Alito's Most Alarming Footnote." *Slate*. Updated May 10, 2022. https://slate.com/news-and-politics /2022/05/the-alarming-implications-of-alitos-domestic-supply-of-infants -footnote.html.

Myong, Lene, and Mons Bissenbakker. "Attachment as Affective Assimilation: Discourses on Love and Kinship in the Context of Transnational Adoption in Denmark." *Nordic Journal of Feminist and Gender Research* 29, no. 3 (2021): 165–77.

Nguyen, Sen. "US Operation Babylift 'Orphans' Are Still Seeking Their Vietnamese Parents, More than 40 Years On." *South China Morning Post*, September 28, 2019.

Patel, Priti. "Forced Sterilization of Women as Discrimination." *Public Health Reviews* 38, no. 15 (2017): 1–12.

Ryan, Mackenzie. "'An Inequality Story': Utah Abortion Ban Will Drive Women Further into Poverty." *Guardian*, July 11, 2022. www.theguardian.com/us -news/2022/jul/11/utah-abortion-ban-women-poverty-inequality.

Shepherd, Sophia. "The Enemy Is the Knife: Native Americans, Medical Genocide, and the Prohibition of Nonconsensual Sterilizations." *Michigan Journal of Race and Law* 27, no. 1 (2021): 89–106.

Smolin, David M. "Child Laundering: How the Intercountry Adoption System Legitimizes and Incentivizes the Practices of Buying, Trafficking, Kidnapping, and Stealing Children." *Wayne Law Review* 52, no. 113 (2006): 115–200.

Sotiropoulos, Karen. "Open Adoption and the Politics of Transnational Feminist Human Rights." *Radical History Review* 101 (2008): 179–90.

Thibeault, Deborah, and Michael S. Spencer. "The Indian Adoption Project and the Profession of Social Work." *Social Service Review* 93, no. 4 (December 2019): 804–32.

Thompson, Ginger. "Court Rules for Deportee on Custody." *New York Times*, June 28, 2009.

Tichenor, Veronica, Julia McQuillan, Arthur L. Greil, Andrew V. Bedrous, Amy Clark, and Karina M. Shreffler. "Variation in Attitudes toward Being a Mother by Race/Ethnicity and Education among Women in the United States." *Sociological Perspectives* 60, no. 3 (2017): 600–619.

Treisman, Rachel. "States with the Toughest Abortion Laws Have the Weakest Maternal Supports, Data Shows." NPR's Reproductive Rights in America series, August 18, 2022. www.npr.org/2022/08/18/1111344810/abortion-ban -states-social-safety-net-health-outcomes.

Wegar, Katarina. "Adoption, Family Ideology, and Social Stigma: Bias in Community Attitudes, Adoption Research, and Practice." *Family Relations* 49, no. 4 (2000): 363–70.

Winslow, Rachel. "Immigration Law and Improvised Policy in the Making of International Adoption, 1948–1961." *Journal of Policy History* 24, no. 2 (2012): 319–49.

Online Sources

African American Policy Forum. "Our Statement on Bodily Autonomy." African American Policy Forum, June 24, 2022. https://www.aapf.org/post/our -statement-on-bodily-autonomy.

Center for American Women and Politics. "Milestones for Women in American Politics." Accessed May 2022. https://cawp.rutgers.edu/facts/milestones-for -women.

Dobbs, State Health Officer of the Mississippi Department of Health, et al. v. Jackson Women's Health Organization et al. 597 U.S. __ (2022). https://www .supremecourt.gov/opinions/21pdf/19-1392_6j37.pdf.

"Document Archives: Jean M. Paton, *The Adopted Break Silence*, 1954." Adoption History Project, Department of History, University of Oregon. Updated February 24, 2012. pages.uoregon.edu/adoption/archive/PatonTABS.htm.

"International Adoption Rate in U.S. Doubled in the 1990s." Population Reference Bureau. Accessed July, 2022. https://www.prb.org/resources/interna tional-adoption-rate-in-u-s-doubled-in-the-1990s/.

Kaelber, Lutz. "Eugenics: Compulsory Sterilization in 50 American States." University of Vermont. Accessed July 19, 2023. https://www.uvm.edu/~lk aelber/eugenics/.

National Association of Black Social Workers. "Position Statement on Transracial Adoptions." September 1972. cdn.ymaws.com/www.nabsw.org/reso urce/resmgr/position_statements_papers/nabsw_trans-racial_adoption_ .pdf.

"People and Organizations: Bastard Nation." Adoption History Project, Department of History, University of Oregon. Updated February 24, 2012. dark wing.uoregon.edu/~adoption/people/bastardnation.htm.

"People and Organizations: Bertha and Harry Holt." Adoption History Project, Department of History, University of Oregon. https://pages.uoregon.edu /adoption/people/holt.htm.

"Topics in Adoption History: Adoption Statistics." Adoption History Project, Department of History, University of Oregon. Updated February 24, 2012. pages.uoregon.edu/adoption/topics/adoptionstatistics.htm.

US Census Bureau. "Living Arrangements of Children: 1960 to Present." Decennial Census, 1960, and Current Population Survey, Annual Social and Economic Supplements, 1968 to 2022. Accessed May/June, 2022. www.census.gov/content/dam/Census/library/visualizations/time-series/demo/families-and-households/ch-1.pdf.

US Department of Health and Human Services. "How Common Is Infertility?" Eunice Kennedy Shriver National Institute of Child Health and Human Development. Accessed May 2022. https://www.nichd.nih.gov/health/topics/infertility/conditioninfo/common.

———. "Recent Demographic Trends in Foster Care." Office of Data, Analysis, Research, and Evaluation. September 2013. www.acf.hhs.gov/sites/default/files/documents/cb/data_brief_foster_care_trends1.pdf.

Film

Blood Memory: A Story of Removal and Return. 2019. Vision Maker Media. https://www.bloodmemorydoc.com.

Dead Men on Furlough. 1954. World Vision, Inc. vimeo.com/37189667.

Index

abandonment of children: fallacy of in transnational adoptions, 85–86, 91–92, 163–65, 176; orphans, deceptive adoption practices around, 33–37, 84–87; "safe haven" laws, 181, 182

ABC News, 164

abductions. *See* coerced/forced child relinquishment

abortion, 5, 33, 122, 155–56. *See also* reproductive rights

abuse, physical and psychological: of adoptees, 157, 177; of birth mothers/families, 46–47, 90–91, 129–34, 141, 180. *See also* coerced/forced child relinquishment

Ackerman, Lillian, 113–14

activism for reform: for adoptee rights and family unification, 147–51, 154–56; against Indigenous adoption practices, 59–61, 66, 156–61; overview, 146–47; against transnational adoptions, 161–65; against transracial adoptions, 45, 151–54

Addams, Jane, 124

addiction behavior. *See* alcohol and drug abuse

Adopted Break Silence, The (Paton), 147–48, 160

Adopted Vietnamese International, 164

Adoptees' Liberty Movement Association (ALMA), 147

"Adoption, Family Ideology, and Social Stigma" (Wegar), 32

Adoption Politics (Carp), 43

adoption records. *See* birth and adoption records; open adoption

adoption regulations and polices, overviews: inadequacy of for transnational adoptions, 162; post–World War II trends, 42–48; Progressive Era state and federal regulations, 37–41, 101–2, 124–25; unregulated programs and practices, 32–37, 79–80

adoptions by proxy, 79–82

adoption trauma, 66, 77–78, 159–61

adoptive family, protection of: emphasis on rights of, 183; through misdirection and deceit, 149–50; through

stigmatization. *See* shame and stigma of adoption; shame of fertility; shame of infertility
suicides in adoptees, 16–17, 122, 159

Taira, Derek, 22
Taking Children (Briggs), 137
tattoos and self-validation, 50, 70–73, 166–67
Taylor, Rosemary, 85–86, 88
teenage mothers. *See* minor/juvenile birth mothers
Temporary Assistance for Needy Families (TANF), 135–37
temporary placement/care lie, 34, 165
Texas Welfare Department, 112
Thibeault, Deborah, 66, 140–41
Third Reich policies, 12–14
Time magazine, 89
transethnic adoption, author's experience, 8–15. *See also* transracial adoptions
transnational adoptions: activism for reform of, 161–65; attachment/assimilation challenges of, 53–54; Chilean Indigenous and Pinochet regime, 90–92; Korean children, 78–83, 90; misrepresentations and deceptions in, 85–86, 91–92, 162–65, 176–77; rates of, 65, 92, 162–64, 180; Vietnamese children, 82, 83–90
transracial adoptions: activism against, 45, 151–54; attachment and assimilation challenges of, 53–54, 59; as cultural genocide, 45; decrease in, 151; narrative of adoptee, 175–79; postwar

trend of, 57–58. *See also* Indian Adoption Project (IAP)
Treikoff, Anecia, 67–68
tribal sovereignty, significance of, 59, 66–67, 159
Trump, Donald J., 140
Truth Will Set You Free, but First It Will Piss You Off! The (Steinem), 186

United Nations Convention on the Rights of the Child (UNCRC), 92, 150, 152–53, 179
United Nations International Children's Emergency Fund (UNICEF), 152–53, 163
University of Hawai'i at Mānoa, 22
University of Washington (UW), 20
unsealing adoption documents, 30, 48, 155, 170
unwed mothers, 116–18, 125–26. *See also* criminalization of unwed pregnancy; illegitimacy
US Children's Bureau (USCB), 37, 79, 89, 124
US Department of Health, Education, and Welfare (HEW), 61
US Department of Health and Human Services (HHS), 138–39
US Department of Homeland Security, 138
US Department of Justice, 140

Vandenhoeck & Ruprecht, Göttingen, 12
Vietnam, adoption of children from, 83–90